IRONMAN's

HOME GYM

H A N D B O O K

*A Complete Guide to
Training at Home*

by Steve Holman

The Home Gym Handbook was written to help you reach your physical potential in the shortest time frame possible. Weight training, however, is a demanding activity, so it is highly recommended that you consult your physician and have a physical examination. Proceed with the suggested exercises, routines and itineraries at your own risk.

ISBN 0-9627834-0-4
Library of Congress Catalog Card Number: 90-85238

Homebody Productions
11693 San Vicente Blvd., Suite 337, Los Angeles, CA 90046

CONTENTS

Acknowledgements

First and foremost I would like to thank my good friend Bill McKnight for planting the seed for this book and helping me to nourish the idea into a publication. I couldn't have done it without him.

I would like to give an emotional "Thanks, Mom" to my mother, Janice Pearlman, for her guidance and for just simply being there when I needed her.

Thanks to my dad, Terry Holman, for showing me the importance of journalistic expression and integrity.

A loving thanks to Becky Holman, my wife and quintessential best friend, for helping me through the ordeals of publishing (not to mention life as a journalist).

Next is John Balik, publisher of *IRONMAN* magazine, whom I thank for his unending support and never-say-die attitude. He's truly an inspiration.

And many thanks to Ben Mall (cover design), Leon Bach (illustrations), Michael Neveux (photography), Jerry Robinson, Randall J. Strossen, Ph.D., Tom Pearlman, Ruth Silverman, Dave Tuttle, Eric Sternlicht, Ph.D., Faith Walker and John Otken for their various contributions, suggestions and moral support.

I would also like to thank those writers in bodybuilding journalism who gave me inspiration and motivation over the years: Jerry Brainum, Arthur Jones, Ellington Darden, Ph.D., Stuart McRobert, Bradley J. Steiner, Dennis DuBreuil and Mike Mentzer.

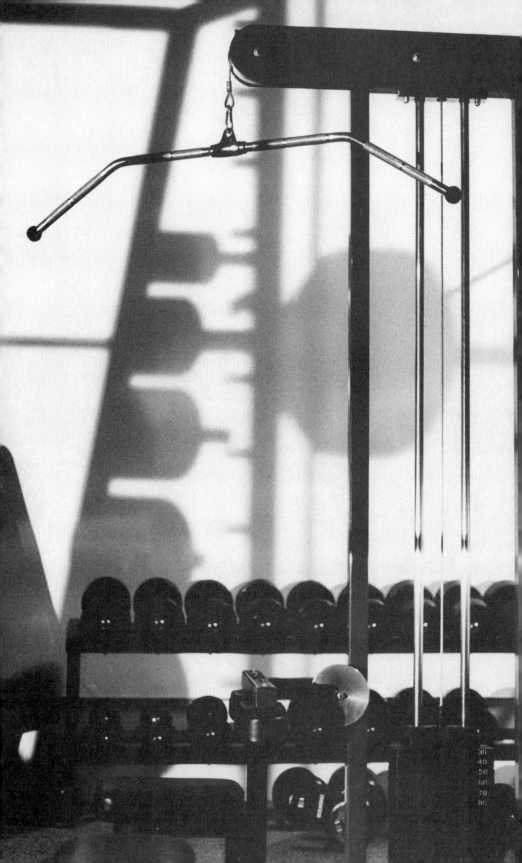

Introduction
Home Sweet Home

Efficiency of effort. These three words form the essence of this book. In a nutshell, efficiency of effort means producing maximum gains with minimal time expenditure; it should be the bodybuilder's bottom line. And, as you will see, there's no better place to accomplish training efficiency than in your very own home.

It doesn't matter whether you're looking for increased muscle mass, strength, power, muscle tone or any combination thereof; your own home gym will allow you to reach your goals with as little waste of both time and money as possible. The actual benefits are overwhelming and boil down to the four Cs of home training: concentration, control, convenience and cost. There's no driving to and from the gym—just walk to the next room (convenience); no waiting for equipment or coping with distractions—you're the only member (control); no interruptions or intrusions—turn on your answering machine and close the door (concentration); no annual membership fee or monthly dues—once you buy equipment, you can use it whenever you want, no charge, and it lasts virtually a lifetime (cost).

Part I of this book gives you all the details you need to set up your own in-house training facility and explains how to maximize the four Cs. It takes you from a basic home gym setup to add-ons that will create the most productive training atmosphere.

"Okay, okay," you're probably saying, "but let's talk results. Can I actually produce great gains in a home gym?" Absolutely! You can make great strides in muscle size and power in a home gym environment, and in many cases the gains will be better than results you could achieve in a commercial gym. Just ask bodybuilders like John Grimek, Bill Pearl and Franco Columbu. These great title winners have all trained for long periods at home—and with spectacular results. In the general fitness world, Jack LaLanne is notorious for his intense home-training sessions. In the field of martial arts, Bruce Lee was a big proponent of home training, and Chuck Norris often pumps a little in-house iron to keep his physique tight and his techniques powerful.

If you're not ready to give up commercial-gym training, do what Lou "The Incredible Hulk" Ferrigno does: Get the best of both worlds—have a commercial-gym membership and a good home gym as well, and let your mood govern when, where and how you work out.

True, there are limitations in the home gym environment, as these champions would all admit; without the various machines and pulley devices found in commercial gyms, the home trainee must be innovative to get the best results possible. This creativity, however, is part of home training's overall appeal. A great workout is only a few resourceful thoughts away: new exercises, a twist of your wrist here, a widening of your grip there, a new intensity technique. This mental challenge makes home training all the more interesting, more satisfying and more productive.

Part II of this book shows you how to make your home gym workouts the best they can be. It cuts through the tremendous amount of misinformation, opinion and sheer nonsense that make weight training appear more complex than it actually is and gives you straightforward, logical facts.

Productive bodybuilding isn't complex, no matter what the "experts" try and make you believe for their own commercial gain (the more complex they make it, the more you need their "expertise"). It's a relatively simple endeavor, but to get the best gains possible, you must understand the basic principles and be able to stand your ground when the various conflicting opinions threaten to stagger your logic or tempt your impatience. For beginner and advanced trainee alike, abiding by the logical guidelines presented in Part II will have you growing from your first few workouts and keep you on an escalating plane until you reach the upper limits of your genetic potential—if that is your goal.

If you've never lifted weights before, Part II will show you how to eliminate the broad trial and error that can lead to wasted time in the early stages of training. By following the ideas outlined, you will gain as quickly as possible—no regrets in the later years of your training career. If you aren't at all familiar with weight training, you may want to review Appendix B, Exercise Descriptions, and the glossary at the end of this book to acquaint yourself with terms and exercise performance.

For the more advanced bodybuilder, the ideas in this book will give you a fresh outlook and put you back on track to rapid progress. You'll find one of the most rational advanced training programs ever developed—the positions-of-flexion routine—and a phase-oriented training itinerary that is unbeatable for creating maximum muscle mass in a short time frame.

This book also includes a complete chapter for the athlete. If you regularly participate in a sport and you're thinking about using weights to enhance your performance, rest assured that proper bodybuilding will increase your speed and power while taking only a fraction of your total weekly training time.

One last point about Part II: Keep in mind that it is not a cookbook, per se. True, there are routines listed and training cycles outlined, but these aren't set in stone. If you try a listed routine and results aren't apparent after a reasonable amount of time, don't hesitate to *slightly* alter your plan of action—just don't stray from the basic principles. As a result, you'll keep trial and error to a minimum and keep the gains coming at a furious pace.

As you will soon see, your home gym is a place where you can max out your physical potential at your leisure without wasting valuable time. Everyone concerned with fitness should have at least a basic home gym. It makes no difference whether you're a hardcore bodybuilder wanting more muscle mass, a business executive itching to build an admirable body or an athlete looking for an edge. The home gym is *the* most efficient tool for helping you achieve your ultimate physical goals.

So enough introduction already. Let's get your home gym and your physique under construction.

Part I
Under Construction: Your Own Home Gym

1

Functional Home Gym Hardware

In the early 1900s, there was an athletic German named Heinrich Steinborn who was serving out his time in the German navy. World War I was going full force, and, as chance would have it, Heinrich's ship was captured off the coast of Australia and brought to port there. During his "capture," Heinrich had nothing to do but work out, think about working out and then work out some more. He quickly outgrew the meager equipment that was in the compound, and before long he was in dire need of some heavier weight.

One day while he was thinking about his predicament, he learned that some trees were being cut nearby to clear some land. Heinrich immediately had a brainstorm. He obtained permission, selected two of the largest stumps that looked to be equal in weight and fashioned a heavy barbell by securing one to each side of a bar. Heinrich used this weight for some heavy-duty workouts during his stay in Australia and became the strongest man around—most of the other men could hardly budge the homemade barbell, much less lift it.

Later in his life Heinrich moved to America, achieved fame for his tremendous feats of strength and became known as the great strongman "Milo" Steinborn, but he never forgot that homemade Australian barbell. It had a special place in his heart because it kept him training and was a symbol of his ingenuity and strength.

Today, we're lucky; we don't have to build barbells out of tree stumps like Milo did just to get a decent workout. With the growing popularity of weight training, the sporting goods stores are overflowing with options for setting up a home gym. It can consist of everything from a simple barbell/dumbbell set and a bench to a wide array of machines, fixed dumbbells and pulley equipment. Let's sift through all of the paraphernalia and start with a basic setup—one that will give you great workouts for the rest of your training career and accommodate add-ons later if you ever want or need more equipment.

Basic Home Gym Requirements

Space. The first priority is a room, porch, patio, garage, basement or small area in your bedroom suitable for lifting. It can be as small as 7' x 7', but try for a 12' x 12' space. This allows for more freedom of movement and extra space for equipment additions later on. Carpet and/or rubber flooring is optional, but it helps keep equipment scuffs and floor dings to a minimum and also reduces the noise level.

Basic weight set. Next, you'll need a good, basic 110-pound barbell/dumbbell set. The best type to buy is either a metal or a rubber-coated metal set. Don't bother with the thick, cement-filled, plastic variety. While they cost less initially, they'll soon crumble, whereas a quality set will last a lifetime. If you are an apartment dweller, do your neighbors a favor and get a rubber-coated set to minimize the banging and clanging.

Extra poundage. After your basic set, you'll want to buy some additional plates. Add four 25s to begin with. This will give you a total weight of 210 pounds, enough for just about any exercise—at least until your strength begins to skyrocket.

Bench. You'll need a good, sturdy, adjustable bench—one that inclines and has uprights (no uprights necessary if you have a power rack or something similar; more on this in chapter 3). This bench should be sturdy enough so that it doesn't topple when loaded with a heavy weight.

A word of warning: Test any piece of equipment, especially a bench, before you buy. You don't have to go through an entire workout in the store showroom, but you can try various movements and check for flaws in construction at all of the major stress points.

One good bench test is to stand on it and slightly shift your bodyweight around. Be careful when you try this, however, as you could get more than you bargained for. If the bench feels like it might flip at any moment, shop around some more.

While stability is of primary safety importance, check also for sufficient padding and bench width. There's nothing more aggravating during a set of bench presses than having your shoulder blades dig into the sharp edges of a poorly constructed bench.

You'll also want a leg extension/leg curl attachment on your bench. While you won't be using it much in the beginning phase of your home-training regimen, it will come in handy as you become more advanced and in need of some boredom-breaking variation. Don't forget to test it, too, for comfort and stability before you lay down your hard-earned cash.

Calf block. A high calf block for doing heel raises is also a necessity. You can make one of these out of an 18-inch 4" x 4" and an 18-inch 1" x 8", which will act as the base. Simply nail the 4" x 4" to the center of the 1" x 8", leaving two inches of 1" x 8" on each side. Then all you need is a heavy dumbbell and a wall to lean against, and you're ready to work calves with one-legged calf raises, one of the best calf builders around.

A high calf block is a home gym necessity for lower-leg work. Be sure your block is high enough to give your calf muscles a good stretch. Four-inches is about right.

Chinning bar. One other useful piece of equipment is a chinning bar. Without a pulldown apparatus, chins are the only effective way to work your upper back from the overhead position. Many sporting goods stores carry a type of chinning bar that you can "wedge" in a doorway. This doorway version is perfect for home gym back work—if your doorway is wide enough—and the bar takes up little room as opposed to a freestanding chinning bar.

Before you go out and spend your money on a chinning bar, however, check the bench in your home gym (or the one you're thinking about purchasing). The uprights on many benches are wide enough and go up high enough so that you can put a barbell bar across them and do chins with your knees bent. This actually isn't as bad as it sounds; you can keep your feet on the ground for stabilization purposes and get a great back workout.

Accessories. Other items on your list should include a lifting belt for back support on heavy exercises, lifting gloves to protect your hands and a weight belt that straps around your waist for adding extra poundage to chins, dips and calf raises. This last item looks like a two-foot piece of leather with a long, detachable length of chain connecting the two ends.

You may be thinking that all of this equipment will wreak havoc with your bank account. Actually once you price each piece, you'll see that it's not that costly to put together an entire home gym. In fact, you'll be surprised at just how inexpensive equipping your gym can be. If you're a little short on cash, you might try placing a want ad in your local newspaper for someone looking to sell.

One last comment: If you decide to go the mail-order route to equip your gym—a decent option for inexpensive equipment—always order products through reputable companies. Ordering from a nonreputable firm can be a nightmare, and what you receive may be nothing like what you saw in the catalog. In other words, you could get a bench that looks like it was assembled by the town drunk. Buyer beware.

Here's a summary of the essentials for an efficient home gym setup:

Home Gym Checklist

- 12' x 12' area (or at least 7' x 7')
- 110-pound metal barbell/dumbbell set (rubber coated, if possible)
- Extra weight (four 25s; this extra poundage is optional for women trainees)
- A comfortable, adjustable bench with uprights and leg extension/leg curl
- Calf block
- Chinning bar (optional for women)
- Lifting belt
- Lifting gloves
- Weight belt (optional for women)

With this equipment, you've got an endless number of muscle-building routines at your fingertips. We'll take a look at some versatile workout strategies in Part II that will get you going and growing faster than you can say "Schwarzenegger," but first let's pump some productivity into your home gym environment.

2

Homemade Productivity

Every trainee, whether home gym enthusiast or commercial-gym diehard, is striving for maximum productivity—the very heart of training efficiency. And achieving maximum productivity has a lot to do with the trainee's environment. Home trainees have a definite controlling edge in this department.

At home, you can essentially create the type of atmosphere that gets you psyched to hit the iron: live music, go-go dancers, strobe lights, fog machines. This list is a bit impractical, which is why it isn't described in more detail, but it does get the main idea across: You're in control. Let's discuss a few useful suggestions on how to up your home gym productivity by taking advantage of this control.

Productivity Tools

The training log. To make the best gains possible with the smallest time expenditure you've got to train smart. And training smart means keeping some sort of training log or diary to monitor your progress. Once again, it's a simple matter of efficiency.

Whether you're training for gargantuan size or just lifting to be a better athlete, you should consider yourself to be a researcher seeking out the most productive techniques available. And what researcher doesn't log his data? Without solid data, an exact science becomes a haphazard procedure fraught with pitfalls and a lot of wasted time—something we're definitely trying to minimize. Here are a few reasons why the training log is an indispensable tool when

The training log is an indispensable piece of equipment that will boost your workout productivity and motivation. It's as essential as the standard lifting belt.

it comes to efficiency of effort:

Progress reference. With a training log, you record your workouts—sets, reps and weight each time you do an exercise. This allows for quick reference in the future so that you can gauge your progress and check for sticking points. You'll be able to tell with a quick flip of the pages what's working and what's not.

For instance, if you look two months back in your log and you're using the same weight on almost every exercise, something is definitely wrong. It may be time to change exercises or take a layoff. Without your training log you might well have missed the telltale sign that something was awry.

Goal-setting tool. The training log can also be used for setting goals. Before going to bed, for example, you might look back and notice your achievements from the previous workout. You can then begin to lock new goals into your subconscious for the following day's workout and put a star by those exercises that might need a poundage increase.

Motivational tool. The training log is more than just a tangible record of your performance or a preworkout goal-setting tool; it can also act as a psychological booster shot *during* your workout. Let's say you're getting ready for a set of squats. Simply look back at your previous day's logged routine and see how many repetitions you got. Perhaps you see 250 x 8 (250 pounds for eight repetitions).

So you get hyped, get psyched and accept nothing less than nine repetitions with 250. Most of the time this preliminary psyching will spur you on to new levels of intensity, creating the ideal stimulus for new muscle growth.

Remember always to strive for more reps and prime your mind to top the previous routine's rep totals. In this sense, the training log is a motivational tool that can't be beat.

Keeping a training log isn't a complicated process. In fact, you have to keep it simple for easy reference. An inexpensive stenographer's pad will do nicely and allow for a quick flip back in time when necessary. Here's a sample entry to give you an idea of how your log should look:

Date:		1/1	1/4	1/9	1/12	1/17
One-legged squat	(set 1)	10 x 10	10 x 12	10 x 14	10 x 15	20 x 10
	(set 2)	10 x 9	10 x 10	10 x 10	10 x 13	20 x 9
Sissy squats		15 x 10	15 x 12	15 x 13	15 x 14	15 x 14
		15 x 10	15 x 9	15 x 10	15 x 11	15 x 11
Stiff-legged deadlift		100 x 11	100 x 11	100 x 13	100 x 15	110 x 11
		100 x 10	100 x 9	100 x 11	100 x 13	110 x 10
One-legged calf		20 x 17	20 x 17	20 x 18	20 x 20	25 x 16
		20 x 15	20 x 14	20 x 16	20 x 17	25 x 14

Notice that the poundage was increased for one-legged squats on 1/17 because the trainee reached the high-rep range (15 reps) on 1/12. The same goes for stiff-legged deadlifts and one-legged calf raises. On sissy squats, however, he didn't reach the high-rep range of 15, so he won't increase the weight until he achieves that goal number (rep ranges for specific exercises will be given in Part II of this book).

Accessory rack . A small peg board on the wall will do wonders for home gym neatness. Here you can hang your lifting belt, gloves, neck strap, weight belt, a clean towel and wrist straps for easy access. No more shifting the entire contents of your gym from one side of the room to the other just to find a buried lifting glove. And no more sifting through the rubble only to find a weight belt pinned under a couple of 25-pound plates, the buckle smashed beyond utility. This organized environment should help boost your workout productivity.

The gym clock. When you first start training with weights, it's okay to go by feel and begin each set when your body and mind are ready. After a month or two of hard training, however, you should begin timing yourself between sets. And what better way to do this than by having a clock with a sweeping second hand on your gym wall, or at least a watch with a stopwatch function?

A 45-second interval between sets should be about right for most trainees. Forty-five seconds is the average recuperation time needed for the muscles of a conditioned athlete to replenish oxygen and remove some of the lactic acid buildup that occurs after an intense set of anaerobic exercise (weight training). Of course, it may take a few weeks for you to work down to this level, but when you do, your workouts will be much quicker and much more productive. (Note: Exercises that use many muscle groups at once—compound movements like squats or deadlifts—may require slightly more rest because of the greater oxygen debt created.)

Bulletin board. Believe it or not, this is one of the essentials of a good home gym simply because it helps pump up your number-one bodypart: your mind.

The first mind-pumping item that should be on your bulletin board is inspirational photos of the type of physique you're looking to emulate. No need to plaster the entire corked area with cutouts; this will only overload your senses. Three or four inspirational shots will do just fine, and you can change them every month or two to give your subconscious some variety.

The next thing that should be on your bulletin board is your specific goals. Once again, don't go overboard and get your mind confused; "A physique that would scare Arnold Schwarzenegger" is not a realistic goal. Go with items like "16 1/2-inch arms," "225-pound bench by Christmas" or "visible gut ruts by summer." These images will help program your mind to achieve what it sees day in and day out.

Last, but not least, a good photo of yourself on the beach or by the pool pinned right next to photos of what you want to look like will do wonders for your inspiration. Compare, don't despair, and then hit the iron with a vengeance!

Full-length mirror. An inexpensive full-length mirror will not only help you keep your form strict, but also motivate you as you watch your bodyparts work and pump out reps. Be sure and put the mirror in a spot where you can see yourself do the majority of your exercises. You'll be surprised at how the image of yourself working can spur you on to higher levels of intensity.

Remember, organization breeds productivity, and productivity in your home gym means bigger size and strength gains in less time. You don't have to turn into Felix Unger from the "Odd Couple," but at least maintain a home gym that helps you maximize your effort and pushes your results above and beyond the average.

Productivity Checklist

_   Training log

_   Accessory rack

_   Gym clock

_   Bulletin board

_   Full-length mirror

3

Home Improvements: Adding On

Everybody is looking for the quick fix—magic gadgets that will help them reach their goal of maximum muscle that much faster. And there are plenty of products around that will supposedly do the trick.

Thumb through any bodybuilding magazine, and you're bound to run across an incredible number of gizmos "guaranteed to pack on muscle mass." Everything from tiny, intricate devices for small muscle groups to huge, machinelike contraptions for complete body fitness is available—for the right price, that is. The question is, how much of this do you really need?

Let's get one thing established here and now: Nothing rivals the good old barbell/dumbbell set for putting on muscle. Ignore the majority of the growth gadgets you see hyped in print; most are designed to reduce your checking account, not build your body.

When you're out shopping around for equipment, your primary concern should be adding to your home gym to make it more efficient by supplementing your basic setup with more barbells, dumbbells and free-weight equipment. By doing this, you make your home gym, as well as your physique, that much more complete. And let's not forget that adding the right pieces of equipment to your gym can do more for your waning enthusiasm than just about anything short of a one-inch gain on your arm measurement.

Here's a list of optional add-ons—when you can afford them—for the basic home gym outlined in chapter one. If you're a beginner or intermediate trainee, none of these items are absolutely necessary; the basic home gym as outlined will do just fine. On the other hand, if you're ready for some heavy advanced training, you won't be able to do without many of these add-ons:

EZ-curl bar. This strategically bent (cambered) bar is a real wrist reliever. If you have problems with wrist pain when doing barbell curls, curling with an EZ-curl bar should put a stop to the excruciation.

But the EZ-curl bar isn't just for biceps work. In fact, it's probably used more for various close-grip triceps extension moves, and for good reason—the grip position in the middle of the bar is perfect for hitting the bulk of the triceps. The bar is also slightly shorter than a regular exercise bar, which makes the close-grip extension movements easier to control, as a close grip on a regular

The EZ-curl bar is an excellent piece of equipment for working the triceps, biceps and forearms.

barbell bar can be hard to balance because of the bar's length. More control with the EZ-curl bar means better pushing leverage, and better leverage means more muscle growth in most cases.

Extra weight. As you get stronger, you'll need more weight to keep gains coming at a steady rate. Adding four 25s (or two 50s) and two to eight 10s, 5s and 2 1/2s should do the trick. You may need more or less depending on your strength level and the other "extras" around the gym you'll want to leave loaded at all times.

Dumbbell bars. Changing the plates on your dumbbell bars can extend your workout time and reduce training productivity. To remedy this, you should buy two to three extra pairs and keep them loaded with frequently used poundages. At commercial gyms, it's usually the 35s through 45s that are missing from the racks, but you may choose whichever poundages you like. Once you've been training for a few months, you can check your log and take note of the numbers that keep showing up on your dumbbell exercises. These are the ones you should have preloaded to make your workout time more efficient.

Barbell bar. The same goes for barbell bars. Buy an extra one and have it loaded with a poundage that you use often. Once again, check your training log.

Dipping bars (optional). Parallel bar dips are considered one of the best arm- and chest-developers in the body business. They can add some variety to chest and triceps work, but they're not absolutely necessary. If you don't have the room or the finances, skip the dipping bars; you can get plenty of development without them. If you're interested in building the ultimate home gym, however, make room in your workout area—and in your budget—for a set. (Note: Some benches have dipping attachments, but check the sturdiness factor before you buy.)

Pulldown machine (optional). Pulldowns are a great substitute for chins, especially if you're not quite strong enough to do chins with your own bodyweight. Once again, however, this is an optional piece of equipment because even if you can't chin yourself, you can always use a chair under your legs to lighten the load until you're strong enough to do them without any help. Even advanced bodybuilders don't really need a pulldown machine, but it is nice for variety's sake. As with dipping bars, the limiting factors are space and money.

Power rack (optional). This is one versatile piece of equipment. It's a rather simple, freestanding structure that can be purchased or, if you're mechanically inclined, built in your own backyard.

The "cage," as it's known in the world of strength, sweat and sinew, looks like an outhouse without any walls—a square base,

The power rack and Olympic barbell set: ideal home gym additions for the advanced bodybuilder.

four support posts (one on each corner) and some support beams at the top. On two of the vertical support posts, there is an adjustable short pin. These two pins hold your barbell bar and can be moved to different heights, up or down, to accommodate just about any exercise from squats to bench presses. There are also two long pins, each running from a front support to a rear support. These "catch" the bar if you miss while squatting or bench pressing inside the cage. They also can be moved up or down through drilled holes in each of the supports.

Whether you've got a home-built model or a steel, store-bought rack, one thing's certain: A power rack, or version thereof, is perfect for the home gym environment. Here are a few reasons why: safety—as mentioned in the description the long pins act as catchers if you miss in a squat or bench press; versatility—you can do everything from squats to bench presses to chins; safety—if you're training for maximum strength, you can set the long pins for partial squats, partial benches or partial deadlifts with complete confidence. This will get you used to the feel of the heavy iron in the power moves (powerlifters virtually eat and sleep in the power rack).

The one problem with the power rack is that it takes up quite a bit of space, so if you don't have a large workout area the cage is out. Advanced bodybuilders would be advised to make room for one or something similar (like squat stands, which are described next); it's a home gym essential when you get big enough to contemplate bodybuilding or powerlifting competition.

Here's a routine using the power rack as a base for each and every exercise. Now that's versatility! (Note: 3 x 12 means three sets of 12 reps.)

Squat	3 x 12
Stiff-legged deadlift	2 x 12
Calf raise	3 x 12-20
Bench press	2 x 8
Incline press	2 x 8
Chinup	2 x 8
Bent-over row	2 x 8
Seated press	2 x 8
Upright row	2 x 8
Close-grip bench press	2 x 8
Curl	2 x 8

Basically, all you need for this routine is a freestanding power rack, a heavy-duty 7' barbell bar (preferably Olympic), plenty of plates and a bench that has the ability to incline (no uprights necessary).

After looking at this routine, you may be asking yourself, "Why do rows and curls in a power rack?" For one simple reason: easy loading and unloading. You put the long pins at about knee level so that the bar is up off of the ground, and breaking down the weight becomes a breeze. With a cage, you'll definitely start to "rack up" bigger and better gains. (Note: Most power racks require an Olympic barbell set because of their width. An Olympic set has a longer bar with larger end sleeves to accommodate Olympic-size plates, which have larger holes through their centers. More in the Olympic set section of this chapter. If an Olympic set isn't feasible, you can still use a power rack along with your standard plates if you purchase a regular 7' barbell bar.)

Freestanding squat stands (optional). Each of these stands is a freestanding upright with its own base. This setup isn't quite as functional as a power rack, but it does have its good points. With the right type of squat stands, an incline bench and a barbell set, you can do a complete routine for your entire body—similar to the one listed in the power rack section. You can put your bar across the squat stands and do chins with your knees bent. You can pull your incline bench between them and you have a set of uprights for incline presses. Flatten out your bench and do bench presses

Squat stands are a good, inexpensive addition to your home gym. Make sure they're sturdy and can hold heavy poundages before you buy. (Photo courtesy of Jubinville Health Equipment.)

with the stands set low and acting as uprights. Your constraints here will be funds; freestanding squat stands cost around $150 per pair, but they take up significantly less space. Just make sure they're sturdy—no wobbling—and adjust to the proper heights before you buy.

Complete home gym training unit (optional). This is the latest addition to the home gym equipment market, and it's a good one. A complete home gym training unit includes a power rack, bench with leg extension/leg curl, pulley system and various attachments. A good one will run anywhere from $1,000 to $2,500, no weights included. That may sound like a lot, but this unit will greatly expand your training options.

If you decide to go the "complete" route, keep in mind that you will need a large space for it; this apparatus can't be tucked away in a corner like the equipment listed in chapter 1 for the basic home gym.

Olympic set (optional). Once again, unless you're closing in on the advanced stage of your weight-training career or considering doing Olympic weightlifting exercises like cleans and snatches, an Olympic set isn't all that necessary. Basically, the only reason to have an Olympic set is its sturdiness. A standard barbell set usually does just fine for most people throughout their training life, even when they're at their strongest.

On the other hand, if you have a power rack and see yourself using some very big weights in the big exercises (squats and bench presses) in the near future, an Olympic set will be a necessity. Of course, you can always start out with the regular barbell setup in chapter 1, and then when you start using close to 300 pounds for squats, bench presses or any of the other big exercises, you can buy an Olympic set with all of the trimmings (or a regular 7' bar) and a power rack and leave your first set for the lighter movements. (Note: If you're going to start out with an Olympic set, you'll still have to buy regular plates to fit your dumbbell bars.)

Here's a rundown of what you might include in your gym once you're on the verge of some serious, advanced training:

The Advanced Home Gym Checklist

- Your first 110-pound metal set (rubber coated, if possible)
- Extra regular plates (two to eight of each: 25s or 50s, 10s, 5s, 2 1/2s)
- Comfortable, adjustable bench (with leg extension/leg curl)
- Calf block
- Chinning bar (a nonessential if you have a power rack or squat stands)
- EZ-curl bar
- Dumbbell bars (two to three pairs)
- Barbell bar (one extra)
- Dipping bars (optional)
- Pulldown machine (optional)
- Power rack or squat stands (optional)
- Olympic set (optional, but suggested for power rack use)

If you're like most home gym trainees, you'll never quit adding to your workout wish list. But remember, always buy quality products, and don't get fooled into buying "magic muscle machines." Nothing beats a good barbell/dumbbell set, so strive to make your free-weight workouts more efficient and less monotonous, and they'll, in turn, become much more effective.

Part II
Strategic Home Training

4

Efficiency of Effort

Terry and Albert were skinny. How lanky were these two high school freshmen? Let's just say they'd both been mistaken for Jolly Roger on more than one occasion and jumping around in the shower to get wet was a common practice. Not only did their arms look like pipe cleaners, but their torsos resembled small, fragile bird cages, every rib standing out in bold relief. And their legs— flamingos would burst out laughing when these two wore shorts.

One day Terry stumbled across his uncle's old weight set while prowling around in his grandmother's attic and decided that this was the way to gain not just bodyweight, but hard, respectable muscle size and strength. He convinced Albert that his find was a gold mine, and with two picnic benches—yes, picnic benches!— homemade squat racks and enough weight to get by with they set out to become muscular marvels capable of winning the Mr. Olympia title with ease and breaking women's hearts with the flex of a biceps.

Well, our slender heroes never made it to the coveted Mr. O (and the hearts they broke weren't nearly as numerous as they had imagined), but they did put on muscular bodyweight—fast! After many cracked patio tiles (sorry, Mom), worn-out picnic benches and rust-stained T-shirts, both Terry and Albert had gained more than 50 pounds apiece *before* they graduated high school, and all of this was accomplished in a makeshift home gym.

The moral of the story: Even with the most basic home gym setup, you should have no problem putting on muscle mass. The key is a flexible workout regimen that incorporates the efficiency-of-effort concept (EOE).

Muscle Growth and EOE

A sensible workout routine will produce dramatic gains for almost any trainee. The routine doesn't have to be complicated or take up tremendous amounts of time. In fact, long, intricate workouts usually make it that much more difficult to achieve muscle growth. On the other hand, if you use a solid, basic routine and push each exercise hard, you are guaranteed to make startling progress.

Pushing each exercise hard means training to "failure," or performing a set of repetitions until another rep is virtually impossible. When training intensely, the last rep of each set (other than warmup sets) should always be a gallant, all-out effort, but one that you can't quite complete.

Let's take barbell curls and run through a set to failure. Pick up a loaded barbell and begin curling. Your first repetition is easy, a slow two seconds up and two seconds down; rep two is a little harder, three a little harder than two and so on, with each rep increasing in difficulty. By rep number seven, you're really struggling to keep your form in tact, but you grit your teeth and manage to crank it out. On rep number eight, you pull hard, keeping your form strict—no back bending or body English—and you stick and then barely make it through the halfway point and up to your shoulders, your biceps shuddering with fatigue. You lower slowly to the count of two, but your biceps are burning so much, each second seems like an eternity. Finally the bar hits bottom and you begin rep number nine, but you don't even make it to the halfway point. Although you pull with all your might and will your biceps to fire through the sticking point, nothing happens. After a few seconds, your mind and muscles simply refuse to budge, so you terminate the set. You've just trained one set of barbell curls to failure. If you model all of your sets after this one just described, you will literally force growth to occur with each workout. Your body has no choice but to cope with the demands you place on it with high-intensity training by growing larger and stronger. (Note: If you train alone, for safety reasons you should perform potentially dangerous exercises like squats, bench presses and stiff-legged deadlifts to just before failure and then stop.)

44

In simple terms, muscle hypertrophy (growth) is merely an adaptation by your body to this stress. Because you are continually increasing, or intensifying, the stress, we call this kind of training progressive resistance. Every time you force your body to go above and beyond what it did previously, your muscles compensate by getting larger and stronger. This translates into bodybuilding's cardinal rule: You must attempt to push your muscular structures harder with each subsequent workout to continue growing past previous levels; no amount of easy training will stimulate inordinate size and strength gains. You must take each set to failure—or beyond—and continually attempt to increase the poundages you use if you're after more muscle mass. You must do this, however, using a routine that will *coax* your body to grow rather than one that throws your body into an overtrained state of shock.

A Strategic Training Schedule

The most productive weight-training regimen in existence is a full-body schedule done on nonsuccessive days during the week. Don't throw up your hands in disbelief and shrug the full-body program off as being only for beginners. True, it's a routine many trainees start out with, but it's also a routine that *all* trainees should return to again and again during their weight-training careers for renewed growth and power, even after they become advanced bodybuilders (more in chapter 7) because, quite frankly, this type of routine is the best raw, basic mass-building routine around.

As the description might indicate, this routine is performed on nonconsecutive weekdays—Monday, Wednesday and Friday, for example—and it works the bodyparts in this order: thighs, chest, back, shoulders, calves, triceps, biceps and abdominals. Because it takes more energy to exercise the larger muscle masses effectively, you do them first, working down to the smaller groups. If you did, say, thighs last in your workout, you most likely wouldn't be able to do them justice, so try and stay with this largest-muscle-groups-first approach except when specializing (specialization is covered in chapter 6). Here's how the model EOE routine looks—a routine that works quite well with the basic home gym setup outlined in chapter 1 (Note: 2 x 8-10 means two sets of eight to 10 repetitions; for exercise descriptions see Appendix B.)

The EOE Routine (Mon., Wed., Fri.)

Thighs	One-legged squat *	
	or barbell squat*	2 x 10-15
	Sissy squat	1 x 10-15
Hamstrings/		
Lower back	Stiff-legged deadlift*	2 x 10-15
Chest	Incline barbell press*	2 x 8-12
	Elevated pushup	
	or barbell bench press	1 x 8-12
Back	Chinup*	2 x 8-12
	Bent-over barbell row	1 x 8-12
Shoulders	Seated dumbbell press*	2 x 8-12
	Wide-grip upright row	2 x 8-12
Calves	One-legged calf raise*	2 x 12-20
	Freehand calf raise	1 x max
Triceps	Lying triceps extension	1 x 8-12
Biceps	Standing barbell curl	1 x 8-12
Abs	Crunch	2 x 15-25

* Do a warmup set with 50 percent of your work weight on these exercises. This won't be possible on some of the movements, so you'll have to improvise. Use the following substitute exercises to warm up with: For one-legged squats, use freehand squats; for incline barbell presses, use regular pushups; for chinups, place your feet on a chair or the floor to lighten the load; for one-legged calf raises, use freehand calf raises. The set numbers listed do not include these warmup sets.

This efficiency-of-effort regimen is a relatively simple schedule, one that can be completed in a little over an hour, and one that will produce immediate and consistent gains for almost any trainee. Other advantages include the following:

- It's easily adaptable to your equipment no matter how basic.

- You work your body as a complete unit, which allows for optimum recuperation.

- You get a day of rest between workouts and two on the weekend; this allows time for often-neglected cardio-vascular training and a more involved stretching program. Keep in mind that it's easier to stick with an exercise program if you do some sort of physical activity—stretching, jogging, walking, etc.—every day.

Also keep in mind that this routine as listed is the *maximum* amount of work (sets) you should do in any one workout and that many trainees will make better progress doing a slightly condensed version of the EOE routine and doing it two days per week instead of three:

Condensed EOE Routine (Mon. & Thurs.)

Thighs	One-legged squat*	
	or barbell squat*	2 x 10-15
Hamstrings/		
Lower Back	Stiff-legged deadlift*	1 x 10-15
Chest	Incline barbell press*	
	or barbell bench press*	2 x 8-12
Back	Chinup*	2 x 8-12
	Bent-over barbell row	1 x 8-12
Shoulders	Seated dumbbell press*	2 x 8-12
	Wide-grip upright row	1 x 8-12
Calves	One-legged calf raise*	2 x 12-20
Triceps	Lying triceps extension	1 x 8-12
Biceps	Standing barbell curl	1 x 8-12
Abs	Crunch	1 x 15-25

* Once again do a warmup set with 50 percent of your work weight on these exercises. This won't be possible on some exercises, so you'll have to improvise: For one-legged squats, use freehand squats; for incline barbell presses, use regular pushups; for chinups, place your feet on a chair or the floor to lighten the load; for one-legged calf raises, use freehand calf raises. The set numbers listed do not include these warmup sets.

Note that this routine includes a total of 16 sets and is done only twice per week to give you more recovery time. If the full EOE program is too much for you, this condensed routine should be about right. Hardgainers—those who are small boned and/or have difficulty putting on muscle—dominate the weight-training world, so don't feel down if you fall into this group and can't tolerate much work. Just be sure you never overtrain; two workouts per week with 10 to 20 total sets per workout will do wonders for the hardgainer.

As Stuart McRobert, renowned *IRONMAN* magazine author and self-proclaimed hardgainer's hardgainer, has said, "I have never gained any size or strength from any routine other than a simple total-body workout done, at most, twice a week." And as Mr. McRobert has advised again and again, if you feel as if you can't handle your present routine, cut back. Even the condensed EOE routine may be too much for you. If that's the case, pare down the sets; do one set instead of two on some exercises, drop direct arm work—whatever it takes. There's no magic set total; just keep your EOE routine in the 10-to-20-total-sets, two-times-per-week range and train intensely, and your gains will start to pile up.

Hardgainers aren't the only people who can benefit from an abbreviated routine, however. This type of training is also effective for the trainee who is participating in another sport one to three days per week (more on bodybuilding for the athlete in chapter 8) and individuals who simply don't have the time and/or energy for the full EOE routine. If you've got a stressful job, a family and/or demanding outside activities, you'll definitely benefit more from the condensed routine or a version thereof. If you're not sure, give the full EOE routine a try. If it makes you feel "wrung out," then switch. Remember, you'll always build more muscle if you stay within the boundaries of your body's recovery capacity.

When it comes to weight training, you are assured of optimal progress if you analyze your body and your lifestyle and then choose the appropriate EOE routine. Both versions work and work fast. To give you a better understanding of the efficiency-of-effort concept and why it works, let's dig a little deeper.

Exercise Analysis: Compound vs. Isolation

If you take a look at the listed routines, you'll notice that most of the exercises are the "big basics," like squats, presses, rows, deadlifts and chins. These movements are the prerequisites when you're going for rapid, drug-free muscle growth and power. They truly adhere to the efficiency-of-effort concept—maximum gains with minimal time expenditure.

The squat, for example, primarily works the frontal thighs but also effectively trains the buttocks, lower back, hamstrings, calves and even the abdominals to a certain extent. Bent-over rows primarily work the upper back but also train the lower back, trapezius, biceps and posterior deltoid. Because they are multi-joint movements, you work a variety of muscles with a single exercise, which is why they are called *compound* and why you only need a few of them to work your entire body effectively and efficiently.

These efficiency-of-effort movements are strong medicine, and they have built more muscle than any machine routine ever could. It is not uncommon for a trainee to gain 20 pounds in the first few months of training. Randall J. Strossen, Ph.D., author of *Super Squats,* claims to have gained 30 pounds of muscle in six weeks using a similar basic routine, and he's a relatively small-boned individual (6 5/8" wrists and 8 5/8" ankles). Most of us would be ecstatic to make one-third of Strossen's gain.

All of the above is not to say that there's something "wrong" with doing isolation exercises—movements that focus on only one muscle group, such as dumbbell lateral raises or leg extensions. Isolation exercises can add growth stimulation to the more advanced trainee's routine—when used strategically, as described in chapter 7 on advanced training. In the beginning, however—during the first year or so of training—a routine dominated by compound movements will produce the optimal efficiency of effort and, therefore, the best gains. The reason for this is the body's early adaptability response, or how our systems cope with intense exercise.

Phase Training and Adaptability

Studies indicate that while a beginner has the ability to increase strength by some 300 percent, his or her ability to recover from the stress of exercise can only increase 50 percent. In other words, the stronger you get, the easier it is to outrun your recovery ability—the ability of your metabolic system to replenish after exercise. Because of this, you should not only use the smallest number of exercises necessary to train your entire musculature effectively (efficiency of effort), but you should also *cycle* your training intensity—how hard you push yourself—in the early stages and throughout your training career to maximize your recovery from exercise. This periodic intensity manipulation is called phase training.

Phase training is simply interspersing periods of all-out training with bouts of moderate exercise. This "hard/soft" approach keeps you from burning out physically and/or mentally. With either of the EOE routines listed previously, you'll be doing 16 to 22 sets to failure in any one workout, and, needless to say, this will be an immense drain on your muscles and nervous system as well as your mental faculties. You'll need to recharge your recovery ability after a number of weeks of high-intensity training, otherwise your gains will stop or—heaven forbid—you may even start losing your hard-earned muscle.

The basis for this phase approach to training is Dr. Hans Selye's General Adaptation Syndrome, discussed in his book *The Stress of Life*. Selye concluded that the human body adapts to any stress in three stages: *alarm, resistance* and *exhaustion*. The alarm stage occurs when you encounter a new stress, such as high-intensity training. In this alarm stage, your body begins adjusting its defenses as it prepares to compensate for the stress.

The next stage is resistance. This is where the adaption actually occurs. In the case of weight training, the resistance stage is where your hard work starts to pay off as muscle growth and strength increase to new levels. But as you push your body harder toward bigger and better gains, things start to taper off, and you eventually reach the third stage, exhaustion, an overtrained state that is detrimental to any athlete's progress. This stage should be avoided for as long as possible.

Properly used, phase training will allow you to sidestep the exhaustion stage for long periods, even when you become more advanced. To help explain this concept further, here's how Selye's General Adaptation Syndrome translates into a phase-training model:

Alarm: Your body fights to adjust itself during the first one to two weeks of high-intensity training.

Resistance (adaption): Three to seven weeks into high-intensity training you grow (adaption).

Exhaustion (overtraining): Your body hits a wall (plateau) eight to nine weeks into high-intensity training.

(*Note:* These estimates are based on the *average* trainee who is using one of the EOE routines in this chapter. Different training approaches, such as the advanced regimen given in chapter 7, may necessitate a slight adjustment in each stage's time allotment.)

With Selye's observations, we can conclude that to avoid overtraining, you should implement a moderate-intensity phase *before* your body kicks into the exhaustion stage, usually around seven weeks into a high-intensity regimen, so that your metabolic system has a chance to catch up and replenish.

Taking all of these facts into consideration, let's take a look at how a beginner would put this information into practice.

In the Beginning

If you're new to weight training or you simply haven't hit the iron for an extended period, you can't just take one of these routines and this training information and start working out full force. You'd get so sore, getting from your bed to the shower would be a painful workout in itself. You'll first want to get a physical examination by a doctor. Then after you get the okay, you'll need a break-in period, which requires some special considerations:

Break-in Itinerary (three-week cycle)

First and second weeks: Do only one set of each exercise (plus warmup) and don't go to failure on any of the sets; stop a few reps short.

Third week: Start training to failure, but keep the sets to one per exercise.

After the third week: It's on to the full routine (either the full EOE routine or the condensed version) and the Beginner's Itinerary.

The Post-break-in Strategy

Once you. the beginner, have completed the break-in period, you'll be primed for some hard and heavy training. Either EOE program will give you the ingredients necessary for muscle growth, and your gains will accrue rapidly as you enter each resistance stage. But don't get carried away and start adding sets and/or exercises. If you do, you'll simply drive yourself into the ground (exhaustion stage), making muscle growth slow if not impossible. The body must be coaxed into growth. This is exemplified by the aforementioned fact that as your strength increases in these early stages so does your potential for overtraining. Taking this into account, here's how a productive beginner's itinerary would look:

Beginner's Itinerary (six-month cycle)

First six weeks: EOE routine; all sets, except warmups, to failure.

Next two weeks: EOE routine; stop all sets one to two reps prior to failure.

Next six weeks: EOE routine; all sets, except warmups, to failure.

Next two weeks: EOE routine; stop all sets one to two reps prior to failure.

Next six weeks: EOE routine; all sets, except warmups, to failure.

Next two weeks: EOE routine; stop all sets one to two reps prior to failure.

If you look closely, you will notice that this is a simple, logical schedule that fits into Selye's General Adaptation Syndrome theory: six weeks of intense training followed by two weeks of moderate-intensity training. This will allow your body's recovery system to alternate between the alarm stage and the resistance stage (growth) for as long as possible.

Even the most advanced trainee, however, can't keep jumping back and forth between stage one and stage two forever. Eventually your metabolic system will balk and slip into the exhaustion stage, which will necessitate a full week off from training. The exact time you hit the exhaustion phase will depend on the individual, so monitor yourself carefully. If you start feeling listless and have little desire to work out, you may have hit exhaustion, which means it's time to take a break from the weights.

Forging Ahead

After six months on this beginner's itinerary, you should be ready for the intermediate itinerary (another six-month phase-training period) complete with specialization (chapter 6), but, again, all of this is relative. Some people may not be ready to make the jump to specialization in only six months. It may take longer, so please don't hesitate to extend the beginner's itinerary for as long as it takes until you're comfortable with progressing into something a little more demanding.

Remember, while beginners do have to cope with some muscle soreness and the trials and tribulations of perfecting exercise technique and learning their bodies, they're lucky in one respect: Progress comes faster than a speeding bullet!

Training Efficiency: Tips and Suggestions

Here are a few training tips you should consider:

- Before you begin any weight-training session, you should do about five minutes of general warming up, including light calisthenics and some stretching of major muscle groups.

- Don't forget your specific warmup sets (done before each asterisked exercise; see the listed routine). A warm muscle contracts harder than a cold one, so what these light preliminaries do is twofold: They get the joints primed for the heavier work to come, and they ready the muscles for better muscular response.

- Repetition speed should be relatively slow—two seconds up and two seconds down.

- Always use a full range of motion. In other words, don't do partial movements; take each exercise from the fully stretched position to full contraction so that the entire length of the muscle is affected.

- If you feel bored with your routine, don't be afraid to substitute other exercises for the ones listed. Substitution movements are listed in Appendix B along with the exercise descriptions.

- If a few exercise changes doesn't do it, you may want to try a whole new routine. Alternate routines are listed in Appendix D.

- Another boredom breaker is to split your routine in half and work out four days per week. For example, on Monday and Thursday, work thighs, hamstrings, calves, chest and triceps; on Tuesday and Friday, work back, shoulders, biceps and abs. (Note: Don't add sets.)

- Rest for one to two minutes between sets.

- Never swing or jerk during a set; when you can't manage another rep using strict form, you've hit *positive failure*.

- Always wear your lifting belt notched tight when attempting heavy poundages in exercises like squats, presses, curls, etc.

- It's best to add weight to an exercise when you reach the higher repetition number listed. For example, in the one-legged squat, add weight when you can do 15 reps. And add enough weight so that you can only get about 10 reps, the lower rep range listed. Then work your way back up to 15 over the course of a few weeks.

- On days when you feel like you're dragging or when you simply don't have the time for your full EOE routine, try doing one set of just the compound movements. This mini-workout will be a nice change of pace and will only take you about 30 minutes.

- If you only have time for one full-body workout during the week, don't fret. Studies indicate that one intense workout is enough to maintain your strength.

- If you belong to a gym, you might want to alternate home training and commercial-gym training. This will provide you with even more variation.

Also, remember that the itineraries in this book are not gospel, but merely flexible models for you to develop your strategy around. You must do everything in your power to avoid overtraining, so don't hesitate to fine-tune your schedule. And if you ever feel as if you need a week off from training, *listen to your body* and take it.

A Few Words for the Women

For women interested in toning, the full EOE routine may be a bit elaborate. It is geared more toward building quality muscle mass fast, not a major concern for most women. (If you do want to build some muscle mass, however, by all means, use it, along with the previously outlined itineraries.)

Women are finally beginning to realize that weight training won't turn them into huge, muscular hulks. It is simply *the* best method for shaping and toning the body. Period.

Here's an at-home routine utilizing the basic home gym outlined in chapter 1 that will do bodyshaping wonders for any woman who

Weight training is the best bodyshaping exercise women can do.

trains consistently and religiously (see Appendix B for exercise descriptions):

Women's EOE Routine (Mon. & Thurs.)

Thighs and buttocks:	Barbell squat	2 x 10-15
Hamstrings and lower back:	Stiff-legged deadlift	2 x 10-15
Chest:	Barbell bench press	2 x 8-12
Back:	Bent-over barbell row	2 x 8-12
Shoulders:	Wide-grip upright row	2 x 8-12
Calves:	One-legged calf raise	2 x 12-20
Abdominals:	Crunch	2 x 10-25

Note: Do one light warmup set—using the bar alone or adding only a little weight—for each exercise (for one-legged calf raises, do regular freehand calf raises).

That's 14 sets to work the major muscle groups—the very things that give your body its shape and curves. Thirty to 40 minutes of exercise two to three days a week for a toned physique—not a bad trade-off.

If it's tone you're after and not muscle mass, you don't have to take your sets to failure (although it's good to do that every now and then—once every two or three weeks for each exercise is about right); the majority of the time simply do repetitions until the set starts becoming uncomfortable, then terminate it.

This program is fast, flexible and works the entire body. It's probably one of the most efficient bodyshaping routines in existence and will provide noticeable improvements in less than one month of steady training. Of course, even the most productive routine can become boring, so here's an alternate workout you might want to use when the first one gets a bit uninteresting:

Women's Alternate EOE Routine (Mon. & Thurs.)

Thighs, buttocks and hamstrings:	Lunge	3 x 10-15
Chest:	Incline bench press	2 x 8-12
Back:	Bent-over one-arm dumbbell row	2 x 8-12
Shoulders:	Barbell military press	2 x 8-12
Calves:	One-legged calf raise	2 x 12-20
Abdominals:	Crunch	2 x 10-25

Try this alternate workout after you've been on the first routine for six weeks. Then after six weeks on this alternate regimen, go back to the first routine for another six weeks. This variety will keep your attitude fresh and your motivation constant.

Once you have diligently followed this type of schedule for four to six months, you'll not only sing the praises of home gym training, but you'll also be ready to specialize on certain bodyparts in order to create head-turning figure illusions—small waist, enhanced bust and smaller hips. More on this in the women's section of chapter 6.

Here are a few tips you should consider when using either of the women's efficiency-of-effort routines:

- Before you begin your weight-training session you should do about five minutes of general warming up, including light calisthenics and some stretching.

- Don't forget your warmup set for *each* exercise. These light preliminaries, done with about 50 percent of your work weight, get the muscles primed for the more concentrated work.

Don't neglect your general warmup routine, which should always precede your weight workout. Five to 10 minutes of stretching and calisthenics will prime your body for the heavier work to come.

- The idea of progressive resistance works for shaping and toning as well as for building muscle. When an exercise feels easy after you reach the prescribed higher number of reps (for example, 12 when the reps are listed as 8-12 and you can do 12 easily), up the weight 2 1/2 to five pounds at your next workout.

- If you have the time and energy for three workouts during any one week, go ahead and do it, training on Monday, Wednesday and Friday. Three-day-per-week training is beneficial every once in a while, but don't burn yourself out; you must do everything possible to maintain a stick-to-it attitude.

- Always use a full range of motion. In other words, don't do partial movements; take each exercise from the complete start to the complete finish so that the entire length of the muscle is affected.

- If you feel bored with your routine, don't be afraid to substitute other exercises for the ones listed. Just be sure your alternate movements work the same muscle groups. Substitutions are listed in Appendix B along with the exercise descriptions.

- Phase training—high-intensity alternated with moderate-intensity phases—isn't necessary unless you're going to failure on your exercises. If you decide you want to try building instead of toning, try the condensed EOE routine along with the beginner's itinerary.

- Average repetition speed should be two seconds up and two seconds down.

- Rest for one to two minutes between sets.

- Never swing or jerk during a set.

- Always cinch your lifting belt up tight for squats, stiff-legged deadlifts, bent-over barbell rows, upright rows and any other movements that stress your back. This will help support your lower back and abdomen.

- Do some type of aerobic activity—jogging, fast walking, tennis, etc.—on the days you don't work out with the weights. You'll find it's easier to stick to a fitness program if you do a little something every day.

Whether you're a teenager who thinks she's too skinny or too fat, a young adult with no muscle tone or an older adult with "loose-skin" problems and underused muscles, weight training is the quick route to a new you. Give it a try; you'll be absolutely thrilled with your results, guaranteed.

5

In-house Intensity Tactics

Whether you train in a lavish commercial gym or a basic home gym, one thing is certain: The more variation you subject your musculature to, the better. Your physique will thrive on new exercises, increased poundages and—the most important for home gym enthusiasts—innovative techniques.

There's no denying that when it comes to exercise variety, the commercial gym, with its many chrome-plated machines and pulley systems, eases ahead of the home gym. But that doesn't necessarily make commercial-gym training better. Far from it. What the home gym lacks in exercise variety, you can make up for with technique innovation. And because these techniques *intensify* your workouts, they will do much more for your ultimate muscular development than the latest space-age machines.

The Intensity Factor

"Intensity" has been tossed around in training circles for years, but many weight trainers still have trouble understanding this concept. Simply turning 12 shades of red during your workout doesn't mean you've trained with intensity and stimulated growth; taking sets to failure and beyond, however, is a good indicator that you have. The bottom line for muscle growth is simple: You must continually push your musculature to new levels if you want it to adapt with increased size and strength.

Many bodybuilders believe that doing more sets will cause this adaption. Unfortunately, the duration of your workout isn't a dominant factor when it comes to muscle growth. Just because a workout is long doesn't mean it will build muscle. In fact, extended workouts cause most trainees to lose muscle due to the rapid onset of overtraining. The only relationship between duration and intensity is that they are mutually exclusive: The harder you train, the less time you should actually spend training if you're trying to build quality muscle mass. Some keen observation bares this fact out.

Notice the stringy quadriceps of any distance runner. These athletes work their thighs at a *low-to-medium intensity level over a long period*. If duration were the key to growth, the winner of the Boston Marathon would have thighs larger than a pair of 50-year-old sequoias.

The thighs of a sprinter, on the other hand, are much closer to bodybuilding standards—large, thick and muscular. The sprinter does few sets (dashes) at top speed (high intensity). He simply cannot do more than a few all-out sprints, or his thighs would completely fatigue with overwork.

All of this considered, why, then, do so many top bodybuilders do workouts consisting of anywhere from 10 to 20 sets *per body-part?* Two reasons: 1) All of the top competitors are genetically superior and have the ability to recover from larger amounts of work than the average person, and 2) many of the top athletes periodically use anabolic steroids to enhance their recovery ability even further, an idiotic practice but still a common one in almost all sports.

High-intensity training is the key to champion bodybuilder Lee Labrada's success. He knows that all-out effort means muscle growth.

Ninety-five percent of those of us who work out with weights should train most of the time with a routine similar to those outlined in chapter 4—the EOE routines—for best results. Slightly longer, more frequent workouts, such as the four-day-per-week advanced strategy coming up in chapter 7, are the upper limit for less-than-superhuman trainees and can be handled for short durations only. All in all, the time/intensity relationship isn't complex: You can work hard, or you can work long, but you can't do both for extended periods.

Intensity Progression

You've probably figured out by now that intensity is the name of the game when it comes to building muscle: The harder you work—up to a point—the more your body goes beyond its previous performance and the more adaption (growth) your body is forced into. But what are some of the ways in which we can cultivate intensity for optimum gains?

Adding weight is one way to increase intensity. As you add weight from workout to workout, your muscles are forced to adapt and get larger. What happens, however, when you're no longer a beginner and you can't add weight on a regular basis? The answer is, you incorporate intensity techniques so that your muscles are forced to continue to adapt and grow in size and strength. Intensity techniques work your muscles in a unique manner that stimulates the body and forces adaption.

Intensity techniques will also help you create muscle pump—the state of the muscle when it is engorged with blood after an all-out set. Although no one knows the actual correlation between muscle pump and growth, the pump appears to be a necessity. If muscle pump wasn't a requirement, then taking the logic of intensity to its conclusion, our ultimate routine would consist of one maximum repetition per exercise—no pump-inducement necessary. Studies indicate, however, that this low-rep style of training does very little for muscle growth. Could it be because muscle pump is absent? No studies are available to substantiate this, but research does suggest that this low-rep style of training affects more of the ligaments and tendons than actual muscle fiber.

Taking your sets to failure—where failure is reached around the eighth repetition on most exercises—will undoubtedly help you achieve muscle pump, while using intensity techniques will help facilitate the process.

Yours truly learned the value of intensity techniques relatively early thanks to a stocky powerlifter named Michael and a bodybuilder by the name of Don. They trained in Michael's home gym, a 15' x 15' building in his backyard that contained nothing but two store-bought benches, a homemade power rack, dipping bars, an Olympic set and some fixed dumbbells.

Michael and Don's workouts were raw basics, but they pushed their bodies hard, and, oh, how they grew. One of the keys to their success was the use of intensity techniques. Michael's favorite was descending sets, or drop sets, as he called them. When Michael would hit failure on any dumbbell exercise, he would immediately pick up a pair of lighter bells and continue to rep out. His effort was awe-inspiring, and what a pump! Sometimes the bodypart Michael was working appeared to grow right before our eyes. I can still picture him cranking out set after set of lateral raises, his delts ballooning up with each subsequent rep.

Don, on the other hand, was a big proponent of forced reps. Whenever he'd hit a sticking point at the end of a grueling set, Michael would apply just enough added assistance to the bar to allow Don to grit his teeth and complete a few more growth-inducing reps. The pain he went through was inspirational to say the least, and the quality muscle he built was phenomenal.

Did their persistence pay off? Well, Michael eventually did some damage in powerlifting meets around the state, and Don won the Mr. Texas title a few years later. All-out, gut-busting intensity undoubtedly played a big role in their achievements.

Home Gym Intensity Techniques

Now that you understand the importance of intensity, here are a few of the best techniques for the home gym environment; please use them with caution:

Unassisted (without a partner)

Descending sets. This doesn't require a partner, but you do need some fast weight reductions or equipment changes for it to work properly. Let's take dumbbell laterals as our example exercise. To use descending sets on any dumbbell movement you need three sets of dumbbells—30s, 20s and 15s, for instance. Do your first set of laterals with the 30s until you can't get another rep, then immediately pick up the 20s and continue repping out. When you reach failure with the 20s, try to endure the muscle ache and continue with the 15s. Your reps will probably decrease with each weight reduction, but you should still get about four to 10 reps on each set.

For barbell exercises, there will be a momentary pause between sets while weight is removed from the bar, but this doesn't lessen the effectiveness to any great degree—if you move fast, that is. To use this technique on curls you might pull a five-pound plate off of each side for the first weight reduction, and take off a 10-pounder from each side for the second.

If you like the look and feel of pumped muscles, the descending-set technique is tailor-made for you. This is actually three sets in one, so use it sparingly for best results.

Pre-exhaustion. With this technique you work the *same* muscle group with two successive sets—one set each of two different exercises. This is known as a cycle. The first exercise is always an isolation movement (single joint—one muscle group used to move the resistance) and the second is a compound movement (multiple joint—more than one muscle group used to move the resistance). By doing the isolation movement first, you *prefatigue* the target muscle, working this muscle without training any other muscles to any great degree. Then, by employing a compound movement, you continue forcing the target muscle to work with the help of the assistance muscles.

To help clarify this principle, here's a list of some useful pre-exhaustion supersets (isolation/compound):

Thighs: leg extensions (isolate frontal thighs)/squats (buttocks brought into play)

Chest: dumbbell flyes (isolate pectorals)/bench presses (triceps brought into play)

Back: pullovers (isolate the lats)/chinups (biceps brought into play)

Deltoids: side laterals (isolate side delt head)/military presses (triceps brought into play)

The rest time must be as close to zero as possible between the isolation and compound movements for best results. (Note: Pre-exhaustion will be the primary intensity technique used in the intermediate specialization routines in chapter 6.)

Rest/pause. This intensity technique is used at the end of a regular set taken to positive failure. Let's take barbell curls as our example. Grab a barbell and do a set of curls to failure. When you can't manage another rep, pause and count to five. Then fire out another rep. Rest another five seconds, then pump out rest/pause rep number two, and so on until you miss.

You should be able to do a total of about three rest/pause reps at the end of your set. Two sets of this and your biceps will be screaming for mercy and pumped to the bursting point. You can use modified rest/pause to up the intensity of any exercise.

Superslow reps. This technique was perfected at Nautilus Sports/Medical Industries for use with their machines, but it works just as well with barbells and dumbbells—if you can handle the growth burn, that is. The primary impetus of superslow reps has to do with form and function. Cheating is literally impossible, and the working muscles get a long, hard, gradual contraction; loose style is impossible.

This technique concentrates on the positive phase (raising) of each rep and really makes your muscles work. Each positive phase lasts between eight and 10 seconds, while the negative (lowering) phase is the normal two seconds. Obviously, your poundage will have to be less than usual—up to a 30 percent decrease. Shoot for four to seven superslow reps during a set. When you can get seven, you should up your weight the next time you do superslow for this particular exercise.

Superslow works especially well on bodyparts that you have trouble feeling. For example, many bodybuilders can't feel their back muscles contracting during chinups. With superslow, however, you can't help but notice which muscles are getting the brunt of the work—they're the ones that feel like they're on fire. Free-hand exercises, like pushups, that you have trouble adding weight to can also be effectively intensified with superslow reps.

1 1/4 reps. Ellington Darden, Ph.D., director of research for Nautilus Sports/Medical Industries, discusses 1 1/4 reps in his book *Super High Intensity Bodybuilding* (Perigee Books, 1986). This technique works best on movements where there is resistance in the contracted position (leg extensions, lateral raises, leg curls, chins, rows, etc.)—you really have to fight to hold the weight in the top position—as opposed to exercises where you can rest in the top position (squats, presses, curls, etc.). The application is simple but effective: Do the positive portion of each rep, up to the contracted position, lower the weight one-quarter of the way down and then drive it back up to the contracted position again before lowering to full extension—the bottom of the movement. You will have to decrease your poundages when you use 1 1/4 reps, but this technique will enhance the growth benefits you derive from the important peak-contracted position—the top of a rep when the working muscles are flexed. Many believe that this contracted position is the most important part of the repetition, so why not work it for all it's worth?

Cheat reps. This was one of Arnold Schwarzenegger's favorite intensity techniques when he was striving for maximum mass in his competitive years. After hitting failure on about the eighth strict rep of an exercise like barbell curls, Arnold would take a few deep breaths and force out a couple more reps with the use of body momentum. The key here is to make the reps hard (remember, the harder you train, the more you gain); don't use so much momentum that the bar flies into the finish position. Also, too much momentum is an invitation to injury, so keep body language to a bare minimum. One to two cheat reps will probably be all you can muster in most exercises.

Assisted (partner required)

Forced reps. Mike Mentzer, 1978 Mr. Universe, popularized this technique and was able to cut his training sessions down to 45 minutes apiece three times a week. Mentzer realized that if your training is more intense, long workouts are detrimental, not to mention impossible.

For this technique, you'll need a partner on most exercises.

When you fail on a regular set (positive failure), your training partner should apply just enough pressure to the bar, dumbbells, etc., so that you can eke out a few more reps. Your partner must make the reps difficult, or the benefits will be minimal at best. (Note: On chins and dips, you can give yourself forced reps by placing your feet on a chair and pushing with your legs just enough to get you through your sticking point.)

Three to four forced reps should be about right for maximum growth stimulation on any exercise, each rep lasting about three seconds maximum, not including the negative, or lowering, portion of the rep. Try not to strain too much on these, or you run the risk of burning too much nervous energy, one of the primary causes of overtraining.

Pure negatives. For these you need a strong partner—one who doesn't mind getting a little extra work simply by helping you. Employing pure negatives means you will only be performing the negative part of each rep—your partner raises the weight for you, leaving the lowering to you. Each negative rep should be slow and controlled—about six seconds apiece. Even with the exaggerated slow movement, you will be much stronger, since you are only doing the negative phase of the movement. Because of this, you should use about 40 percent more weight during these pure negative sets to really overload the muscles.

The theory behind this technique is a logical one: With pure negatives, you are overloading the muscle, and so you have the potential to involve more muscle fibers during this phase of the movement. But be prepared for some soreness the next day; negatives stress everything from muscle fiber to connective tissue.

As a side note, you can also use negatives in combination with forced reps at the end of a set of positives. For example, once you hit positive failure on triceps extensions, have your partner help you force out three or four reps, then have him lift the weight into the top position for each of three to four negative reps—you perform the lowering only. Talk about intensity! Your triceps, or whichever muscle group you're working, will feel like they've been blowtorched.

Isometric stops. This technique was popularized by Ray Mentzer, Mike's brother and the 1979 Mr. America. For these, you do a regular set to failure, have your partner help you with a few forced reps, then have him raise the weight to the top position for negatives. Instead of lowering all the way down in one continuous motion, however, you stop the bar one-third of the way down, two-thirds of the way down and close to the bottom. At each of these positions along the range of motion, you drive hard, attempting to reverse the movement of the barbell, dumbbells or whatever for three seconds. Your partner should prevent any upward movement by applying pressure to the bar, if necessary, in each position. Contrary to popular opinion, these isometric contractions give a muscular boost to both size *and* strength gains.

The Health for Life Training Advisor, edited by, Andrew T. Shields, M.D., discusses a study that appeared in the *Journal of Applied Physiology* (Volume 64, No. 4, 1988) involving isometric exercise. Three groups of men were studied for five weeks. Group one trained their biceps isometrically at 25 degrees (0 degrees is full extension), group two trained their biceps isometrically at 80 degrees (just below the halfway point), and group three trained their biceps isometrically at 120 degrees (near full contraction).

All subjects showed strength increases throughout the range of motion—not just in the position trained. The group that attained the highest increase throughout the range of motion was group one, the group that trained the isometric contraction closest to full extension. The conclusion: Isometrics is an effective mode of training and can be a productive adjunct to regular weight training. (To obtain a copy of *The Health for Life Training Advisor*, see the chapter on suggested readings at the end of this book.)

Remember, don't go overboard with any of these intensity techniques, or you might accidentally lock yourself into the overtraining dungeon—not an easy place to escape from by any stretch of the imagination. To help you avoid the dungeon, here are a few tips on how to use these intensity techniques effectively and efficiently:

Be frugal. This can't be emphasized enough. It's very easy to get carried away with these techniques. While they can produce gains rather rapidly, try to avoid the more-is-better syndrome. Remember, when it comes to intensity, a little goes a long way. Use these techniques judiciously and intelligently, and you will get bigger and stronger much faster.

You might, for example, choose *one* bodypart per week and do all exercises for that bodypart using a variety of the aforementioned techniques. Then go to positive failure only on all of your other bodyparts. The next week, choose another bodypart to intensify, and go to positive failure on all of the rest. Then the next week choose another bodypart, and so on.

Another technique is to choose one set of one exercise per bodypart and incorporate an intensity technique on each of these sets during a given week. This way every muscle group gets the benefits of intensity for one tough set, but because you're only intensifying a low total number of sets—around eight—you will successfully avoid overtraining.

Intensity Application

However you incorporate them, use intensity techniques only in your all-out phases. Ten sets, or about half of your set total, should be your limit, and most of the time you should do less. Also, refrain from using any intensity techniques whatsoever in the first four months of the beginner's itinerary. After that, work them in slowly.

Be creative. Most of these techniques lend themselves to combinations. You might like to try some of the following combos:

- Use forced reps at the end of each descending set.

- Do rest/pause on your last descending set.

- After a five-to-10-second pause, crank out some regular-speed (two-seconds-up, two-seconds-down) forced reps at the end of a superslow set.

- Do 1 1/4 reps on your last descending set.

Variation breeds size and power, so vary your sets often but don't get carried away, and steer clear of triggering your body's exhaustion stage (overtraining).

Monitor yourself. If your muscles are constantly sore and/or you get nervous "shakes" during the day, you're probably overtraining. Other symptoms include high resting pulse rate and restlessness during the night. If you notice any of these signs, cut back on the use of intensity techniques immediately.

Log your techniques. For reference, use abbreviations in your training log (N for negatives; SS for superslow, etc.) designating the intensity technique used next to the appropriate set. This will help you discover what works best for you, how much intensity your body can handle and what exercises haven't had the intensity treatment for a while.

Take breaks. Every so often, you should go through a week or two without using any intensity techniques whatsoever. If you are following the itineraries in this book, these moderate workout weeks are provided for. This is phase training—your recovery system is allowed to catch up and heal, which helps you avoid overtraining (exhaustion stage). If you're training on a modified itinerary you designed yourself, please don't forget these necessary phases of moderate exercise, or you may compromise your gains.

Just to give you an idea of how a workout would look with an appropriate number of intensity techniques worked in, here's a sample training log entry during one of the all-out intensity phases. (Note: 30 x 12 means 30 pounds for 12 reps.)

Monday	
One-legged squat	30 x 12
	30 x 10 (+ forced reps)
Sissy squat	20 x 15
Stiff-legged deadlift	180 x 10, 9
Incline dumbbell press	65 x 9 (+ rest/pause)
	65 x 7
Barbell bench press	185, 165, 135 x 8, 6, 4 (desc. set)
Chinup	body x 8 (superslow)
	25 x 8
Bent-over row	135 x 10
Seated dumbbell press	45 x 9, 8
Wide-grip upright row	80 x 9 (1 1/4)
	95 x 10
One-legged calf raise	40 x 15, 12
Freehand calf raise	body x 30
Lying triceps extension	80 x 9 (+ isometric stops)
Standing barbell curl	100 x 6 (+ 2 cheat reps)
Crunch	25 x 12, 11

The weights used in this routine are merely hypothetical; taking the schedule as a whole, however, you can get a good idea of how to work in these techniques to intensify your own effort. Also notice that only seven sets are "intensified," which is a nice, medium figure not likely to trigger overtraining.

Hardgainers should never exceed seven intensity sets and most of the time should stay on a routine much shorter than the one listed on the previous page. Here's a sample hardgainer's routine with an appropriate number of intensity techniques:

Monday

Squat	185 x 12
	185 x 10 (+ rest pause)
Stiff-legged deadlift	145 x 10
Incline barbell press	135 x 9 (forced reps)
	135 x 7
Chinup	body x 4 (superslow)
	10 x 8
Bent-over row	125 x 10
Seated dumbbell press	35 x 9
	35 x 8
Wide-grip upright row	70 x 9 (1 1/4)
One-legged calf raise	35 x 15
	35 x 12
Lying triceps extension	70 x 10
Standing barbell curl	85 x 10 (+ 2 cheat reps)
Crunch	25 x 15

As a side note, to make sure you don't get carried away, you may want to sit down and plot where you will use these techniques for a week's worth of workouts at a time. This strategic workout development can be motivationally stimulating and get you psyched for your next workout.

By using intensity techniques you'll be able to make your home gym workouts more intense, more productive and much more interesting. Hit your workouts hard, but use moderation, and you'll reap the fastest bodybuilding rewards possible.

EQUIPMENT INFORMATION GUIDE

NEW YORK BARBELL
P.O. Box 3473
Elmira, NY 14905-0473
benches, racks, plates, bars
Color catalog $2
(607) 733-8038 or 1-800-446-1833

JUBINVILLE HEALTH EQUIPMENT
P.O. Box 662
Holyoke, MA 01041
benches, racks, plates, bars
Write for catalog

TK STARR
201 S. 2nd Ave.
Mt. Vernon, NY 10550
benches, racks, pulley systems
Write or call for brochure and prices
(914) 667-5959

WATE-MAN MANUFACTURING, INC.
26325 Northline Rd.
Taylor, MI 48130
benches, racks, pulley systems
Write or call for catalog
(313) 946-7072 or 1-800-526-0707

UNIVERSAL BODYBUILDING, INC.
32458 Dequindre
Warren, MI 48092
benches, plates, bars, supplements,
books
Write for catalog

IRONMAN *PRODUCTS*
13348 Beach Ave.
Marina del Rey, CA 90292
weight sets, bars, plates, benches, accessories
Write for price list

KITS
54 Stewart St.
Sharon, PA 16146
Build your own equipment. Materials
supplied, you provide the labor.
Catalog $2: 1-800-245-KITS

SPARTAN MFG.
1719 Grant St., Suite 1
Santa Clara, CA 95050
Ironmaster home gym systems
Free catalog: 1-408-988-4002

KUC'S FITNESS
P.O. Box 215
Mountaintop, PA 18707
all types of heavy-duty equipment
Write or call for information
(717) 823-6994

ROYAL HOUSE
P.O. Box 4332
Monroe, LA 71211
benches, bars
Free catalog
(318) 323-0956

SCHISLER INTERNATIONAL
7034 Worthington-Galena Rd.
Worthington, OH 43085
benches, pulley systems, bars
Call or write for catalog
1-800-762-4549

FITMAR ASSOCIATION
6063 Frantz Rd., Suite 103
Dublin, OH 43017
benches, complete and partial home
gym units, accessories.
Free catalog: 1-800-669-0041

6

Specialization: Homing In on Your Weak Points

At some point in time—usually after about six months of steady training—a trainee may want to begin specializing. Each and every one of us has a bodypart or two (or three or four) that doesn't quite respond like the rest. These stubborn stragglers cause trauma and heartbreak for bodybuilders from every walk of life, especially those who have competition aspirations. Nothing throws a person's symmetry off like a lagging bodypart. (Picture a bodybuilder with arms that look like 20-pound hams and thighs that resemble buggy whips, and you'll get the misproportioned picture.)

For those of us who work out for athletics or physical well-being and have no intention of competing, the stubborn muscle group isn't as threatening, but it can still cause some hazardous strength imbalances. For example, many athletes pull their hamstring muscle because their frontal thigh muscles are so much stronger than their hams that their underdeveloped, less-flexible hamstrings can't cope and thus get injured.

Understandably, then, you shouldn't ignore the idea of specialization. And as with any procedure, there's a right way and a wrong way to specialize.

Just Add Sets, Right?

The incorrect way to specialize, in most cases, is to simply do more for the lagging bodypart—so much more that your system goes into overtraining shock. No thought, no strategy, just jack up the number of sets. Even the most advanced bodybuilders have made this mistake. True, the lagging bodypart is begging for a little extra volume, but you obviously shouldn't give it so much more work that your muscle growth slows or even stops.

Ellington Darden, Ph.D., relates a story about Arthur Jones, the creator of Nautilus machines, in his *Nautilus Bodybuilding Book* (Contemporary, 1982) that gets this excessive volume problem across quite well:

In the early 1950s Jones tried various bodybuilding routines in an attempt to find the one that worked best for him. He was never fond of wasting time, so he wanted a system that produced the fastest gains possible. He settled on a routine very similar to the three-day-per-week EOE routine listed in chapter 4, *but with more sets*. His regimen consisted of 12 basic barbell exercises done for *four* sets each (48 total sets), and all sets were taken to positive failure.

With this style of training, Jones' bodyweight peaked at 172 pounds. For 15 years he sporadically trained in this fashion—usually in his home gym—and his bodyweight never exceeded 172. Needless to say, he wanted to be bigger, but his body just didn't seem to want to grow anymore.

Was this 172 pounds the extent of his genetic potential? He was beginning to think just that, so he decided to cut his set total in half, thinking he would simply maintain his muscular bodyweight. He performed only two sets of each exercise (24 total sets).

To his amazement, he gained almost 10 pounds within one week, and his strength level increased above his previous best. Jones was stunned. He learned an important lesson about weight training: His longer workouts had been stimulating growth all right, but they hadn't been allowing growth to happen. Don't let yourself fall into this overtraining trap, especially when specializing.

Work Harder, Not Longer

The correct way to specialize is to work the lagging muscle group harder while increasing the volume for that part *ever so slightly* and *decreasing overall volume*. This will prevent you from overtaxing your system and still produce enough of a "jolt" to your lagging bodypart to stimulate new growth.

Using the EOE routine, let's modify it for a lagging bodypart so that you can get an idea of the proper way to specialize. To review, here's what the EOE routine from chapter 4 looks like:

Mon., Wed., Fri.

Thighs	One-legged squat	
	or barbell squat	2 x 10-15
	Sissy squat	1 x 10-15
Hamstrings/		
Lower Back	Stiff-legged deadlift	2 x 10-15
Chest	Incline barbell press	2 x 8-12
	Elevated pushup	
	or barbell bench press	1 x 8-12
Back	Chinup	2 x 8-12
	Bent-over barbell row	1 x 8-12
Shoulders	Seated dumbbell press	2 x 8-12
	Wide-grip upright row	2 x 8-12
Calves	One-legged calf raise	2 x 12-20
	Freehand calf raise	1 x max
Triceps	Lying triceps extension	1 x 8-12
Biceps	Standing barbell curl	1 x 8-12
Abs	Crunch	2 x 15-25

That's 22 sets, not including warmup sets, approximately the maximum number most trainees should attempt in any one workout. Now, when incorporating a specialization routine, we must keep the set total at 22 or preferably fewer. (Remember, avoid overtaxing the recovery system at all costs.)

For our example, let's say you're having problems with your shoulders (deltoids); they're just not getting that round, full look every bodybuilder craves. That means it's time to specialize. Here's what your new routine with delt emphasis would look like:

Mon., Wed., Fri.

Delts	Barbell military press	2 x 8-12
	Lateral raise	2 x 8-12
	cycled with*	
	Dumbbell upright row	2 x 8-12
Thighs	One-legged squat	
	or barbell squat	1 x 10-15
	Sissy squat	1 x 10-15

Hamstrings/		
Lower back	Stiff-legged deadlifts	1 x 10-15
Chest	Incline barbell press	1 x 8-12
	Elevated pushup or barbell bench press	1 x 8-12
Back	Chinup	2 x 8-12
	Bent-over barbell row	1 x 8-12
Calves	One-legged calf raise	2 x 12-20
	Freehand calf raise	1 x max
Triceps	Lying triceps extension	1 x 8-12
Biceps	Standing barbell curl	1 x 8-12
Abs	Crunch	1 x 15-25

Note: Do a warmup set for each bodypart using the first exercise for that bodypart and 50 percent of the work weight for that exercise.

* A cycle is when you follow the first exercise with a second exercise, taking no rest in between—in this case lateral raises immediately followed by dumbbell upright rows for a pre-exhaustion effect. After the second exercise, take a 45-second rest before repeating the cycle.

Let's take a look at the things that were altered from the original routine, so that you get a better understanding of exactly how to specialize.

Priority. The first thing we did was move the lagging bodypart to the beginning of the routine. This allows you to work your weakest area when your energy and enthusiasm are highest. The only time you wouldn't move the bodypart to the beginning of the routine is if biceps or triceps were the "chosen" bodypart(s). Specializing on either of these first would negatively affect other exercises later in the workout (pressing would suffer because of prefatigued triceps, and pulling movements like chins and upright rows would suffer because of prefatigued biceps). If you want to specialize on biceps or triceps, it's better to keep them at the end of the session.

Variation. We also changed exercises for the sake of variety and to create a new growth stimulus for the lagging bodypart: Seated dumbbell press switched to barbell military press, and barbell upright row changed to dumbbell upright row with a preliminary set of lateral raises. This latter superset—doing an isolation movement prior to a compound exercise—is an example of pre-exhaustion, a real muscle-scorching intensity technique.

Pre-exhaustion. As discussed in chapter 5, this intensity technique dictates that you use a single-joint movement (isolation) to prefatigue a major muscle group before going to a multiple-joint movement (compound) for that same muscle group with no rest. This pre-exhaustion cycle increases the intensity dramatically and produces a full, muscle-numbing pump.

In the example, the strength of the biceps is brought into play with the upright rows (compound) immediately after the lateral raises (isolation) in order to push the deltoids harder. This not only creates an enormous pump, but also increases the work load exponentially.

Pre-exhaustion may seem somewhat complicated, but it's really not once you grasp the inherent theory behind the principle. Even so, you don't have to understand the inner workings of this technique to use it successfully. All you really need to know is how to properly work the specialization routines that appear later in this chapter into your training regimen without triggering your exhaustion stage.

Bodypart volume increase. The next change we made was a *slight* increase in sets for the lagging bodypart. This is to ensure maximum muscle-fiber fatigue. Notice that the total sets for deltoids went from four to six, not a huge increase but an effective one nevertheless, as long as intensity is high on every set.

Overall volume decrease. While we slightly increased the number of sets for deltoids, the *overall* number of sets went from 22 to 20. Why is the set total two notches lower? Primarily because of intensity. By using pre-exhaustion for the deltoids, you are increasing intensity and burning more of the body's reserves (recovery ability), and thus the total number of sets should be reduced to compensate. Do reduce your sets; remember Arthur Jones and his 172-pound sticking point.

Specialization Routines

Now that you have a general understanding of specialization and intensity, here are a few routines for you to choose from in your quest for proportion, symmetry and balance (Note: For exercise descriptions see Appendix B):

Thighs
Barbell squat 2 x 10-15
Leg extension 2 x 8-12
   cycled with
Alternating lunge 2 x 8-12

Hamstrings
Leg curl 2 x 8-10
   cycled with
Stiff-legged deadlift 2 x 8-10

Chest
Dip 2 x 8-12
Incline flye 2 x 8-10
   cycled with
Incline barbell press 2 x 8-10

Back
Bent-over barbell row 2 x 8-12
Barbell pullover 2 x 8-10
   cycled with
Behind-the-neck chin 2 x 8-10

Shoulders
Military press 2 x 8-12
Lateral raise 2 x 8-10
   cycled with
Upright barbell or dumbbell row 2 x 8-10

Calves
Standing calf raise 2 x 12-20
   cycled with
Toes-pointed leg curl 2 x 12-20

Triceps
Lying triceps dumbbell extension 2 x 8-10
   cycled with
Dip (elbows in) 2 x 8-10

Biceps
Seated dumbbell curl 2 x 8-10
   cycled with
Undergrip chin 2 x 8-10

Forearms
Wrist curl 2 x 8-10
   cycled with
Reverse curl 2 x 8-10

Abdominals
Crunch 2 x 15-25
   cycled with
Reverse crunch 2 x max

These are potent routines, so use them intelligently and remember not to specialize haphazardly. For more specialization routines, you can take the individual advanced bodypart sessions in chapter 7 and work them in—no more than one at a time—to your EOE workout, as we did with the delt specialization routine earlier in this chapter. (Note: Women should do one set instead of the recommended two on each exercise in the listed routines.)

Intermediate Specialization Itinerary

After six months of training on the beginner's itinerary listed in chapter 4, you may want to modify it slightly to incorporate specialization for your second six months of training if you have a lagging bodypart or two. If not, continue with the beginner's itinerary for the second six months, but incorporate intensity techniques during the six-week all-out phases. (Note: Advanced trainees will use the specialization itinerary as well, so don't skip over this; it's important to understand the techniques involved.)

If you do decide to specialize, here's how your second six months would look. (Note: For the complete training itinerary, see Appendix C.)

Intermediate Itinerary (Second Six Months)

First four weeks: Work specialization into your EOE routine for your weakest bodypart. Intensity techniques can also be used sparingly throughout the routine.

Next two weeks: Back to the normal EOE routine; stop each set short of positive failure.

Next four weeks: Specialization on a different weak bodypart. Intensity techniques can be used sparingly throughout the routine.

Next two weeks: Back to the basic EOE routine again; stop each set short of positive failure.

Next four weeks: Specialization on a weak bodypart. Intensity techniques can be used sparingly throughout the routine.

Next two weeks: EOE routine, stop each set short of positive failure.

Next four weeks: Specialization on a weak bodypart. Intensity techniques can be used sparingly throughout the routine.

Next two weeks: EOE routine; stop each set short of positive failure.

At the end of your second six months (one year of training) it will be time to determine if you're ready for the advanced training regimen in the next chapter.

If you compare this intermediate itinerary to the beginner's itinerary in chapter 4, you'll notice that the all-out intensity phases have been shortened to four weeks instead of six. The reason for this is that, during the intermediate itinerary you will be using intensity techniques in a more liberal fashion as well as using recovery-draining specialization routines. This combination can cause overtraining (Selye's exhaustion stage discussed in chapter 4) to occur five to six weeks into the high-intensity phase rather than eight to nine weeks into it, as in the beginner's itinerary. By shortening the intensity phase, you can circumvent the extreme drain on your recovery system and avoid overtraining for a longer period of time.

Remember, when it comes to specialization, there must be a method to your madness, namely sculpting your physique into a symmetrical, powerful whole with a phase-oriented training strategy.

Tips on Specializing

- Don't worry about specialization until you have at least six months of solid training under your belt.

- When specializing, work a lagging bodypart harder with only a slight increase in volume for that bodypart. *Overall* set volume should *decrease*.

- Always specialize on only one bodypart at a time, or your overall set total will be too high.

- Feel free to substitute exercises. Replacement movements are listed in Appendix B along with the exercise descriptions.

- Go ahead and use some intensity techniques during your specialization routine where appropriate. For example, on the delt routine mentioned earlier, do some rest/pause reps on presses, take laterals to positive failure and then do 1 1/4 reps on upright dumbbell rows. You can use intensity techniques throughout the rest of your routine, but be careful. Ten sets with intensity techniques should be your absolute ceiling, and most of the time do less. Keep in mind that pre-exhaustion is an intensity technique in itself, so always monitor your progress. Overtraining is something you want to avoid like the plague!

Illusionary Specialization for Women

The novice female home gym enthusiast will immediately realize the tremendous bodyshaping potential of weight training: results appear in rapid fashion. And just like any home gym trainee, she may want to begin specializing after the preliminary six months of steady training.

Most women, however, don't have the desire for bodypart "proportion" as defined by the bodybuilder. They are more interested in developing the classic hourglass figure with a little muscle tone thrown in for good measure.

If that last sentence describes you, you'll be more than a little interested in illusionary specialization, a strategy perfected by Vince Gironda, a respected gym owner (Vince's Gym in North Hollywood, California) and bodybuilding authority, to de-emphasize your genetic body flaws and create the appearance of a better figure. You accomplish this by developing certain bodyparts in order to create a figure illusion, so to speak. Here are the bodyparts you would specialize on—following the specialization suggestions in this chapter—to emphasize certain aspects of your hourglass shape:

If you have a wide waist and/or hips, specialize on and develop your shoulders (deltoids) and your back to make your lower torso and hips appear smaller.

If you have sweepless, "bird legs," specialize on calves and thighs. Do your thigh exercises with feet together for more concentration on the outer thighs.

If you have overly skinny arms, add some arm work *at the end of your EOE toning routine* (chapter 4)—one to two sets of curls and lying triceps extensions should be sufficient. (Note: Because the women's routine has an overall set total that is lower than normal, it's acceptable to specialize by simply adding sets.)

If you have a small or sagging bust line, specialize on your chest to tone the muscles underneath the breast tissue and specialize on your back to enhance your posture.

If your buttocks tend to be flat and/or sagging, do two sets of regular barbell squats instead of one-legged squats for more gluteal (buttock) emphasis.

Once again, try to specialize on only one bodypart at a time. Ideally, to emphasize your hourglass shape, you would follow this type of scenario:

First four weeks: Specialize on your shoulders to de-emphasize waist and hip width.

Next two weeks: Go back to your basic EOE routine.

Next four weeks: Specialize on your back.

Next two weeks: Go back to your basic EOE routine.

Next four weeks: Shoulder specialization or specialize on another bodypart.

Here's how your routine might look if you decide to specialize on back for four weeks:

Mon.-Wed.-Fri.

Back	Chinup (with help, if necessary)	1 x max
	Barbell pullover cycled with	1 x 8-10
	Bent-over barbell row	1 x 8-10
Thighs and buttocks	Squat	2 x 10-15
Hamstrings/		
Lower back	Stiff-legged deadlift	2 x 10-15
Chest	Barbell bench press	2 x 8-12
Shoulders	Wide-grip upright row	2 x 8-12
Calves	One-legged calf raise	1 x 12-20
Abdominals	Crunch	2 x 10-25

Note that sets were reduced from two to one on the one-legged calf raise to compensate for the one additional set on the back specialization routine.

One last point for the women: Take the sets in each specialization routine (three sets in the example) to positive failure—where one more repetition is impossible—most of the time. This will ensure development and help you accomplish the figure illusions you're after faster and more efficiently.

It really makes no difference whether you're a woman wanting better curves or a bodybuilder whose symmetry needs a little something extra, the strategy is the same: specialize. Simply analyze your body, determine what part needs some extra attention and adjust your workout accordingly to coax it into new growth.

7

Advanced Home Training

The word "advanced" is a relative term. In bodybuilding circles it's used to denote someone who competes in the sport, while average weight trainers often use it when referring to anyone with more than a few years of training experience. For our purposes, "advanced" describes any trainee who has mastered the basic movements and has had some experience manipulating a basic routine, like the EOE regimen, with substitution exercises and perhaps specialization. This level of expertise is usually reached after about one year of steady training.

After this "year of discovery," you will be well-versed in many of the exercises that are possible in your home gym, and you will also have a good understanding of how your body responds to certain training intensities and routines. In fact, you will have probably made adjustments to correspond with these findings.

With at least one year of training on your workout resumé, the time has come to make a decision: You must determine whether you want to continue on with the intermediate itinerary with periodic specialization or take a leap forward with a more advanced routine. Your choice will depend on how you have progressed so far and, of course, your goals.

If you're training for athletics or you work a demanding job, the intermediate itinerary (specialization), or a version thereof, is probably all you'll have time for (more on this in chapter 8). Or, if you're training just to look great with that healthy, athletic aura, the intermediate itinerary, with its periodic specialization, will allow you to reach your desired physical development without stealing too much of your time.

On the other hand, if you want to take your musculature to the limit—with full, *complete* development in all of the major muscle groups—you'll want to graduate to a more multi-angled approach to training, but you'll want to do this in an efficient manner.

Advanced Analysis

Look at any top bodybuilder's routine and you'll see that he or she has incorporated a variety of movements for each bodypart. The theory behind this is that each muscle group must be worked from as many different angles as possible to ensure full, complete development.

The problem with most of these routines, however, is that there's simply too much overlap—many of the same angles are worked in one specific bodypart routine—for example, a delt routine might include the military press and the seated dumbbell press; both work the shoulders in a similar manner.

What many bodybuilders end up doing is incorporating a variety of movements for each bodypart without giving much thought to a strategy. This "shotgun approach" is effective, to a degree, but not very efficient, especially if you are a natural bodybuilder trying to avoid the overtraining bullet.

Remember, efficiency of effort requires thought and analysis, and if we analyze the specific movements available for each muscle along with how that muscle functions, we can come up with a much better strategy for reaching full, complete development. This strategy is called the positions-of-flexion (POF) approach.

The Positions-of-Flexion Approach

Basically, each muscle has three positions of flexion: the stretch position, the midrange position and the fully contracted position. If we work each muscle through all three of its positions with enough intensity, the result will be massive, full development.

To help you better understand POF, let's take the triceps as an example and determine its three positions of flexion:

- The *stretch* position of this muscle is achieved when your upper arm is up next to the side of your head and the lower arm is bent back behind it, knuckles almost touching your shoulder, as in the bottom position of a standing triceps extension.

- The *midrange* position is where your arms are out in front of your torso, as in the bench press. Lying triceps movements work this position effectively.

- The fully *contracted* position of the triceps is achieved when your arms are down next to your sides, straight (elbows locked) and slightly back behind your body (the muscle is fully flexed). This position can be worked with triceps kickbacks or one-arm pushdowns.

If you work these three positions hard, your triceps are guaranteed to blow up beyond recognition during any given workout. You should work all of your muscle groups through their individual three positions of flexion if you're interested in achieving advanced muscle mass in the shortest time frame possible. Here's a rundown of each position of flexion for the major bodyparts:

Thighs (quadriceps)

Midrange: squatting or leg-pressing type movements.

Stretch: bottom of a sissy squat—torso and thighs on the same plane, with calves flush against the hamstrings.

Contracted: top of a leg extension—torso and thighs at a right angle, lower legs extended and knees locked.

Hamstrings

Midrange: the middle-to-top portion of a stiff-legged deadlift.

Stretch: bottom one-third of the stiff-legged deadlift.

Contracted: top of a leg curl—torso and thighs on the same plane, with calves flush against hamstrings and feet flexed toward the shins.

Calves (gastrocnemius)

Midrange: toes-pointed leg curl.

Stretch: bottom of a donkey calf raise—calves stretching off of a high block, toes pointing slightly inward, knees locked and torso at a right angle to the legs.

Contracted: top of a standing calf raise—up on toes, torso and legs on the same plane and toes pointed slightly outward.

Upper Chest (pectoralis minor)

Midrange: incline press movements.

Stretch: bottom of an incline flye—elbows down behind, and almost perpendicular to, the torso.

Contracted: extended arms crossed over upper chest.

Lower Chest (pectoralis major)

Midrange: any flat-bench press or decline press.

Stretch: bottom of a decline flye—elbows back behind torso.

Contracted: extended arms crossed over lower chest.

Back (latissimus dorsi)

Midrange: front chin or front pulldown movement.

Stretch: bottom of a pullover—upper arms overhead with elbows slightly below the plane of the torso.

Contracted: bottom of an undergrip chin or undergrip pulldown—upper arms down, behind the torso.

Midback (midtrapezius)

Midrange: behind-the-neck chin.

Stretch: bottom of a cable row or bent-over row—torso forward, bent at slightly less than 90 degrees to the thighs, arms extended.

Contracted: top of a cable row or bent-over row—elbows back behind torso and angled slightly away from the body and shoulder blades together.

Abdominals

Midrange: standing presses, squats, etc.—worked during all movements that require you to hold your torso upright.

Stretch: bottom of a Roman-chair situp—too dangerous to work, especially if you have a genetically weak abdominal wall; hernia could result.

Contracted: top of a crunch—sternum pulled toward pelvis.

Shoulders (primarily the lateral, or side deltoid head)

Midrange: overhead pressing movements.

Stretch: bottom of a one-arm incline lateral raise—arm across the front of the torso.

Contracted: top position of an upright row to nose level—upper arm out to the side and angled slightly upward.

Triceps

Midrange: lying triceps extension.

Stretch: standing overhead extension.

Contracted: dumbbell kickback or one-arm triceps pushdown.

Biceps

Midrange: upper arm is slightly in front of the torso, as in the standing barbell curl.

Stretch: bottom of an incline dumbbell curl—upper arm is straight, down and back behind the plane of the torso.

Contracted: upper arm is next to your head, forearm flush against the upper arm, palm down and little finger twisting outward. This position is hard to simulate with any conventional barbell exercise, but nonsupport concentration curls will get you as close as possible.

Forearms (flexors: underside)

Midrange: undergrip chin, curls, etc.—worked by the gripping involved when performing other exercises, like chins, curls, rows, etc.

Stretch: bottom position of a wrist curl with bench angled slightly upward.

Contracted: top position of a wrist curl with bench angled slightly downward.

Forearms (extensors: top of lower arm)

Midrange: reverse curl.

Stretch: bottom position of a reverse wrist curl with bench angled slightly upward.

Contracted: top position of a reverse wrist curl with bench angled slightly downward.

The POF Home Gym Routine

With the explanations in the previous section, you've probably got the makings of a good routine bouncing around in your mind. And if you've really thought about it, you have probably realized that some exercises work two of the three positions of flexion. This makes some exercises more efficient than others and provides an economy of motion that can help preserve your recovery ability— in some cases, you only need two exercises to work a bodypart's

90

three positons of flexion. For example, stiff-legged deadlifts work the hamstrings' midrange *and* stretch positions.

Let's take a look at the ultimate advanced home gym routine. This routine is done four days per week (Note: M = midrange, S = stretch and C = contracted):

POF Four-day Split

Monday & Thursday

Thighs	Squat (M)	2 x 10-15
	Sissy squat (S)	2 x 10-15
	Leg extension (C)	1 x 10-15
Hamstrings	Stiff-legged deadlift (M&S)	2 x 10-15
	Leg curl (C)	1 x 10-15
Calves	Leg curl (toes pointed) (M)	2 x 12-20
	Donkey calf raise (S)	2 x 12-20
	Standing calf raise (C)	1 x 12-20
Upper chest	Incline press (M)	2 x 8-12
	Incline flye (S&C)	2 x 8-12
Lower chest	Dip or bench press (M)	2 x 8-12
	Decline flye (S&C)	2 x 8-12
Triceps	Lying extension (M)	2 x 8-12
	Overhead extension (S)	1 x 8-12
	Kickback (C)	1 x 8-12

Tuesday & Friday

Lats	Front chin (M)	2 x 8-12
	Barbell pullover (S)	2 x 8-12
	Undergrip chin (C)	1 x 8-12
Midback	Behind-the-neck chin (M)	2 x 8-12
	Bent-over row (S&C)	2 x 8-12
Delts	Behind-the-neck press (M)	2 x 8-12
	Incline one-arm lateral raise (S)	2 x 8-12
	Wide-grip upright row (C)	2 x 8-12
Biceps	Barbell curl (M)	2 x 8-12
	Incline dumbbell curl (S)	1 x 8-12
	One-arm concentration curl (C)	1 x 8-12
Abs	Crunch (C)	2 x 15-20

This four-day-per-week routine will give your muscles new stimulation and renewed growth with about 20 to 26 sets per workout. Even the trainee with below-average genetics—a.k.a. the hardgainer, about 60 percent of those who take up weight training—can benefit from this regimen for short periods of time (four-week intervals or less).

For those of you with above-average genetic potential (larger bones, put on muscle fairly easily, etc.—definitely the minority) here's a three-day split routine that is a bit more extensive; use it as either a three-days-on, one-off routine (preferred) or a six-days-on, one-off schedule.

POF Six-day Split

Day 1

Thighs	Squat (M)	3 x 10-15
	Sissy squat (S)	2 x 10-15
	Leg extension (C)	2 x 10-15
Hamstrings	Stiff-legged deadlift (M&S)	3 x 10-15
	Leg curl (C)	2 x 10-15
Calves	Leg curl (toes pointed) (M)	2 x 12-20
	Donkey calf raise (S)	2 x 12-20
	Standing calf raise (C)	2 x 12-20

Day 2

Upper chest	Incline press (M)	2 x 8-12
	Incline flye (S&C)	2 x 8-12
Lower chest	Dips (elbows wide) (M)	2 x 8-12
	Decline flye (S&C)	2 x 8-12
Lats	Front chin (M)	2 x 8-12
	Barbell pullover (S)	2 x 8-12
	Undergrip chin (C)	2 x 8-12
Midback	Behind-the-neck chin (M)	2 x 8-12
	Bent-over row (S&C)	2 x 8-12
Abs	Crunch (C)	3 x 15-20

Day 3

Delts	Behind-the-neck press (M)	3 x 8-12
	Incline one-arm	
	lateral raise (S)	2 x 8-12
	Wide-grip upright row (C)	2 x 8-12
Triceps	Lying extension (M)	2 x 8-12
	Overhead extension (S)	2 x 8-12
	Kickback (C)	1 x 8-12
Biceps	Barbell curl (M)	2 x 8-12
	Incline dumbbell curl (S)	2 x 8-12
	One-arm concentration curl (C)	1 x 8-12
Forearm flexors	Incline wrist curl (S)	1 x 8-12
	Decline wrist curl (C)	1 x 8-12
Forearm extensors	Reverse curl (M)	1 x 8-12
	Incline reverse wrist curl (S)	1 x 8-12
	Decline reverse wrist curl (C)	1 x 8-12

POF Routine Notes

1) The order of work for each bodypart should remain midrange first, stretch second and contracted position third. The most dangerous position of the three is the stretch; therefore, this movement is done *after* the muscle is warmed and worked by the midrange exercise. The contracted position is worked last because this movement is best for "finishing off" the muscle; working a muscle in the contracted position will deplete more of the muscle's remaining glycogen (energy) reserves.

2) Without a cable crossover apparatus, the chest's contracted positions (upper and lower) are hard to affect. Therefore, when you do incline and decline flyes, make a concentrated effort to flex the pecs hard for two seconds at the top of each rep.

3) For the forearm routine (not included in the four-day advanced routine), the best way to incline or decline your bench is by elevating the end with the calf block described in chapter 1 or with a 4" x 4" block of wood. For inclines, use the end with the block under it; for declines, use the other end.

4) If you feel like you need extra sets, fight the urge to add them. Twenty-four or so is the maximum set total you should use for any one workout.

5) Try to make each set a little different from the last with altered foot positions, slightly narrower or wider hand positions, etc. This will provide for even more variation.

6) If you're not quite ready for an advanced routine, each of the aforementioned bodypart routines can also be used as specialization schedules. For example, you could work the positions-of-flexion thigh routine into the three-day-per-week EOE routine if you wanted to specialize on your thighs. Just remember to follow the specialization procedures in chapter 6 along with the intermediate (specialization) itinerary.

7) Foot positions are always on the trainee's mind when working calves. The contracted position necessitates a toes-out finish at the top, while the stretch position requires a toes-in position at the bottom. Try rotating your foot *ever so slightly* during each rep of standing and donkey calf raises—toes in at the bottom, toes out at the top. Some people find this difficult and may want to do one set toes-in style and the second set toes-out style for both donkey and standing calf raises.

8) Concerning grip positions, keep in mind that a narrower grip on compound movements (bench press, behind-the-neck press, etc.) allows a greater range of motion but forces more assistance from other muscle groups. A wider grip works the target muscle more directly, but the range of motion is decreased. Because of this, a medium grip is the preferred compromise, but you should still *slightly* vary your grip from set to set for added stimulation.

9) The reason biceps, triceps and forearms receive less sets than most of the other bodyparts is because of indirect work: The biceps get worked in most pulling movements (chins, rows, etc.), the triceps get worked in all of the pressing movements (dips, bench presses, etc.), and the forearms get worked in all of the exercises requiring gripping and/or hanging (chins, curls, presses, etc.).

10) If you've been training for more than one year on a routine more extensive than the EOE routine, you should take a full two weeks off before attempting either of these advanced routines. This will give your recovery ability a chance to heal because, all things considered, you're probably overtrained. After your layoff, take one of the above routines and follow the advanced itinerary outlined in the following section.

Advanced Phase Training

The positions-of-flexion advanced routine gives you a maximum of 24 sets per workout, and each session can be completed in approximately one hour. That's efficiency, but that's also still quite a few sets, especially considering the fact that you're working out more often than three days per week. If you were to use either of these advanced routines continuously, you would undoubtedly slam into the overtraining wall before too long (Selye's exhaustion stage, discussed in chapter 4). To ward off the overtraining syndrome and make your advanced strategy as productive as possible, you need to use, once again, a phase-oriented approach. Here's an advanced itinerary most trainees will find productive (Note: For a look at all the training itineraries, see Appendix C):

Advanced Itinerary (4 1/2-month cycle)

First four weeks: advanced routine, all sets to positive failure only.

Next two weeks: advanced routine; stop each set before positive failure.

Next four weeks: advanced routine with intensity techniques (used sparingly).

Next two weeks: advanced routine; stop each set before positive failure.

Next four weeks: advanced routine with intensity techniques (used sparingly).

Next two weeks: advanced routine; stop each set before positive failure, or you may want to take a complete layoff if you're feeling somewhat burned out at this point in time.

After you have completed the entire cycle, begin to alternate itineraries, as follows:

Next four months: intermediate itinerary—two-to-three-day-per-week specialization training for this 16-week period.

95

Third four months: advanced itinerary—four- or six-day-per-week POF training.

And so on, continually rotating the intermediate and advanced itineraries every four months, with a one-to-two-week layoff whenever you feel you need it.

Once again, a four-week intensity phase alternated with a two-week moderate phase will keep you fluctuating between the alarm and resistance (adaption) phases for as long as possible.

And speaking of phase training, you may be wondering why the all-out phases in this advanced itinerary are the same and not shorter than the four-week periods in the intermediate (specialization) itinerary. The reason for this is that your recovery ability should now be developed enough to handle the slight increase in the work load that four-day-per-week training requires. Nevertheless, always monitor yourself for symptoms of overtraining. If you feel yourself getting drained during one of the four-week intensity phases, by all means jump into the moderate phase early, cut back on the use of intensity techniques and/or reduce your overall set totals.

POF Flexibility

The position-of-flexion routine is based on logic (the three positions of muscular contraction) and maximum productivity (phase training), but flexibility is also one of its cornerstones. For example, if you find another chest routine in a bodybuilding magazine or book that you'd like to try, drop the positions-of-flexion chest routine, and work the other one in during one of your four-week intensity phases. Watch your overall set total though; don't let it get above 24 (you may have to cut back the sets on other bodyparts to compensate).

For even more variation, try using some of the pre-exhaustion specialization routines from chapter 6 as substitutes for the various positions-of-flexion routines during your intensity phases. Do, however, come back to the POF routines the next time around because, without a doubt, the positions-of-flexion approach is one of the best advanced training strategies ever devised.

8

The Home-field Advantage

Two decades ago weight training was taboo for almost all athletes. Coaches believed it would make an athlete slow and tight—muscle-bound, as they called it. If a coach found out an athlete was training with weights behind his back, that athlete was reprimanded severely.

Today coaches encourage their athletes to train hard and heavy with the iron. In fact, many pro football teams give monetary incentives to get players into the gym in the off-season to build quality muscle because, quite frankly, it's obvious that powerful players win football games by manhandling opponents. It's also obvious that weight training is the quickest avenue to this awe-inspiring power.

But it's not just football players who are benefiting from the power-building properties of pumping iron. Athletes in every realm are discovering the weight-training edge. Even race car drivers are hitting the weights to help them gain more control over their machines on the track.

Sound Strength Training

Athletes spend countless hours each week practicing their chosen sport. It can be time consuming and mentally exhausting, but many are still willing to make time for weight training in their schedules because of the overwhelming performance-enhancing effects.

Athletes who ignore weight training simply don't realize the benefits or don't have an efficient strategy. They think it takes at least two hours, six days per week in the gym to get results. Actually, about *two hours a week total* in a convenient home gym is all it takes. You just need motivation, commitment and the right training strategy.

The Athlete's Training Strategy

No matter which muscles are predominantly used in your particular sport, you should still train with an *overall* body routine similar to one of the EOE routines outlined in chapter 4. Because of the heavy demands that specific sports training subjects the athlete's body to every week, however, you will have to modify the weight-training routine: Two days per week will almost always be more productive. You should also reduce the total number of sets so that your metabolic system is not overtaxed to the point of burnout. Let's take the EOE routine from chapter 4 and alter it to fit the serious athlete's schedule.

Athlete's EOE Routine (Mon. & Thurs.)

Thighs	One-legged squat*	
	or barbell squat*	1-2 x 10-15
Hamstrings/		
Lower back	Stiff-legged deadlift*	1-2 x 10-15
Chest	Incline barbell press*	
	or barbell bench press*	1-2 x 8-12
Back	Chinup*	1-2 x 8-12
	Bent-over barbell row*	1-2 x 8-12
Shoulders	Seated dumbbell press*	1-2 x 8-12
	Wide-grip upright row*	1-2 x 8-12
Calves	One-legged calf raise*	1-2 x 12-20
Abs	Crunch	1-2 x 15-25

*Do a warmup set with 50 percent of your work weight on these exercises. This won't be possible on some exercises, so you'll have to improvise: For one-legged squats, use freehand squats; for incline dumbbell presses, use regular pushups; for chinups, place your feet on a chair or the floor to lighten the load; for one-legged calf raises, use freehand calf raises. The set numbers listed do not include these warmup sets.

Notice that your set total can range anywhere from nine to 18. Which exercises you use two sets on and which you use one set on are strictly up to you. If you're having a particularly exhausting week training for your sport, drop all sets down to one. If you're coasting in your sports training, do the full routine. It's that simple; just use your best judgment and go by how you feel.

You may want to go back and look over chapters 4 and 6 again; everything said in those two chapters applies to the athlete, except that you will be training two days per week on a slightly different program. Here's a complete itinerary for the athlete who has never lifted weights before but is ready to take advantage of home weight training:

Athlete's Itinerary

Break-in Phase

First two weeks: athlete's EOE routine, one set per exercise (plus warmup), stop each set before positive failure.

Third week: athlete's EOE routine, one set per exercise, go to positive failure on each set other than warmups.

Beginner's Phase *(first six months)*

First six weeks: athlete's EOE routine, set total up to required number (nine to 18), go to positive failure on each set other than warmups.

Next two weeks: athlete's EOE routine, stop each set before positive failure.

Next six weeks: athlete's EOE routine, go to positive failure on each set other than warmups.

Next two weeks: athlete's EOE routine, stop each set before positive failure.

Next six weeks: athlete's EOE routine, go to positive failure on each set other than warmups. Can also begin using intensity techniques—on not more than four total sets per workout.

Next two weeks: athlete's EOE routine, stop each set before positive failure.

Intermediate Phase *(six months and beyond)*

First four weeks: specialization routine incorporated into athlete's EOE schedule for a chosen bodypart. Go to positive failure. Intensity techniques can also be used—sparingly.

Next two weeks: athlete's EOE routine, stop all sets before positive failure.

Next four weeks: specialization routine incorporated into athlete's EOE schedule for a chosen bodypart. Go to positive failure. Intensity techniques should also be used—sparingly.

Next two weeks: athlete's EOE routine, stop all sets before positive failure.

Next four weeks: specialization routine incorporated into athlete's EOE schedule for a chosen bodypart. Go to positive failure. Intensity techniques should also be used—sparingly.

Next two weeks: athlete's EOE routine, stop all sets before positive failure.

If you are already training with weights, the break-in and beginner's phases aren't necessary. You can plunge right into the intermediate (specialization) phase and continue with it indefinitely or until the iron bug bites you and you get the urge to try the advanced itinerary in chapter 7.

One last point: When you work with the intermediate phase, specialization isn't always necessary. You can use the normal athlete's EOE routine with intensity techniques during the four-week all-out phases once in a while instead of specializing. Specialize only when you feel that it's necessary.

Sports Analysis

Before you, the athlete, can specialize, you must first decide which muscles you rely upon most in your sport. Observe the movements you make—for a cyclist, pushing the pedals; for a swimmer, pulling through the water, etc. From this analysis, you should be able to determine which muscle groups are most important to your specific sport. Here are a few examples:

Tennis and racquet sports
Forearms: grip, wrist rotation

Shoulders: forehand, backhand, power serve

Chest: forehand, power serve

Back: backhand, power serve

Cycling
Lower back: torso support in bent-over position*

Forearms: grip, maneuvering (mountain biking especially)

Thighs: hill climbing, passing

Calves: hill climbing, passing

Martial arts
Calves: thrusting forward for power punching, quick bursts of movement, footwork

Thighs: Kicking (snap extension), quick bursts of movement

Shoulders: punching, blocking, grappling

Chest: punching, blocking, grappling

Back: punching, blocking, grappling

Forearms: punching, grappling, weaponry

Abdominals: torso movement and stabilization; taking a punch

Swimming
Shoulders: first two-thirds of the downward stroke through the water

Chest (minor involvement): first two-thirds of the downward stroke through the water

Back: full stroke through the water

Triceps: last one-third of downward stroke

Thighs: kicking

Skiing (downhill)

Calves: ankle torsion

Thighs: shock absorption, maneuverability

Lower back: torso movement and stability*

Abdominals: torso movement and stability

*There are no specialization routines listed for the lower back. To give this area more concentration, leave stiff-legged deadlifts where they are in your EOE routine, add one to two sets and reduce your overall set total to compensate.

Just because a muscle group appears in the list under your sport doesn't necessarily mean you must specialize on it. The martial artist, for example, may feel that his or her calves and thighs are fine and require no additional work. There's no need to specialize on strong bodyparts.

With a good handle on how your musculature is involved in your sport activities, you're now ready to specialize.

Specialization for the Athlete

It isn't difficult to incorporate specialization into the athlete's EOE routine. Here's a step-by-step review of the specialization procedures detailed in chapter 6:

1) Decide which muscle group you want to give extra attention.

2) Put the specialization routine for this bodypart at the beginning of your workout (see chapter 6 for specific routines; the individual advanced bodypart routines in chapter 7 can also be used for specialization purposes). If your chosen bodypart is biceps, triceps or forearms, insert them at the end of your workout to prevent inhibiting other movements in your routine.

3) Delete the specific exercises for this bodypart from

the rest of the EOE routine. For example, if you insert a thigh specialization routine at the beginning of your routine, take one-legged squats out of the remainder of your routine.

4) Cut back on the sets for the bodyparts that you don't use much in your sport until your set total is 18 or lower. (If you're not training very intensely for your sport, you don't have to cut back your set total; simply insert the specialization routine at the beginning of your routine; never, however, go over 22 total sets).

5) Use your "new" routine for four weeks, with intensity techniques here and there, then go back to your regular EOE routine for two weeks, stopping each set before positive failure.

6) The following four weeks after your two-week moderate-intensity phase, go back to step 1) and choose a different bodypart to specialize on.

Weight training will give the athlete performance-enhancing power.

Let's take the cyclist and develop an itinerary for working specialization into this athlete's EOE routine.

First and foremost, the athlete must analyze the sport involved and determine which muscles he or she relies upon the most. After the break-in and beginner's itineraries, the cyclist will want to specialize on thighs, calves, forearms and lower back; these are the important bodyparts in cycling. Here's how the cyclist's training specialization itinerary would look:

Cyclist's Intermediate Itinerary

- *First four weeks:* Incorporate a thigh-specialization routine into your EOE program as follows.

Mon. & Thurs.

Thighs	Barbell squat	2 x 10-15
	Leg extension	2 x 10-15
	cycled with	
	Alternating lunge	2 x 8-12
Hamstrings/		
Lower back	Stiff-legged deadlift	2 x 10-15
Chest	Barbell bench press	2 x 8-12
Back	Chinup	2 x 8-12
	Bent-over barbell row	1 x 8-12
Shoulders	Seated dumbbell press	2 x 8-12
	Wide-grip upright row	1 x 8-12
Calves	One-legged calf raise	1 x 12-20
Abs	Crunch	1 x 15-25

(Note: Even with the addition of more sets for thighs, the rest of the exercises were adjusted so that the set total remains at 18.)

- *Next two weeks:* Go back to the standard athlete's EOE routine (sets terminated before failure).

- *Following four weeks:* Incorporate a calf-specialization routine as follows:

Mon. & Thurs.

Calves	Standing calf raise cycled with	2 x 12-20
	Toes-pointed leg curl	2 x 12-20
Thighs	Barbell squat	2 x 10-15
Hamstrings/		
Lower back	Stiff-legged deadlift	2 x 10-15
Chest	Barbell bench press	2 x 8-12
Back	Chinup	2 x 8-12
	Bent-over barbell row	1 x 8-12
Shoulders	Seated dumbbell press	2 x 8-12
	Wide-grip upright row	2 x 8-12
Abs	Crunch	1 x 15-25

(Note: Once again the set total remains at 18.)

- *Next two weeks:* Go back to the regular athlete's EOE routine.

- *Following four weeks:* Work in a forearm specialization routine, as follows. Remember, the forearm routine must be added to the *end* of your routine because if worked earlier, it would tire the forearms, which would inhibit the working of other muscle groups.

Mon. & Thurs.

Thighs	Barbell squat	2 x 10-15
Hamstrings/		
Lower back	Stiff-legged deadlift	2 x 10-15
Chest	Barbell bench press	2 x 8-12
Back	Chinup	1 x 8-12
	Bent-over barbell row	1 x 8-12
Shoulders	Seated dumbbell press	1 x 8-12
	Wide-grip upright row	1 x 8-12
Calves	One-legged calf raise	2 x 12-20
Abs	Crunch	2 x 15-25
Forearms	Wrist curl cycled with	2 x 8-10
	Reverse curl	2 x 8-10

- *Next two weeks:* Go back to the standard athlete's EOE routine, but stop all sets one to two reps short of failure.

- *Following four weeks:* Specialize on your lower back. Here you will add sets to the lower-back exercise and reduce your overall set total.

Mon. & Thurs.

Thighs	Barbell squat	2 x 10-15
Hamstrings/	Stiff-legged deadlift	3 x 10-15
Lower back	Barbell bench press	2 x 8-12
Back	Chinup	2 x 8-12
	Bent-over barbell row	2 x 8-12
Shoulders	Seated dumbbell press	2 x 8-12
	Wide-grip upright row	1 x 8-12
Calves	One-legged calf raise	2 x 12-20
Abs	Crunch	2 x 15-25

- *Next two weeks:* Go back to the standard athlete's EOE routine, stopping all sets one to two reps short of failure.

Now you can repeat the entire itinerary or work with the athlete's EOE routine as is for a while without any specialization. If you choose the latter, do still employ phase training (four to six weeks of high intensity followed by two weeks of moderate intensity) so that you don't overtrain.

As you can see, specialization doesn't involve mind-boggling scientific theorems. It's basically a simple procedure involving a sensible strategy. For the athlete, this means deciding which muscle groups are used in his or her particular sport and then giving these bodyparts the home gym attention they need to develop the ultimate athletic edge.

9

The Weight-free Workout

Here you are stuck in a hotel room in a strange town. There isn't a barbell or dumbbell for miles—at least none you know about—and your body seems to be losing muscle tone and size by the minute. You need some kind of exercise, something that will be intense enough to give the old musculature a good going over.

Calisthenics? Nah, you need something with some resistance. Calisthenics reminds you too much of high school P.E. anyway. So what's a desperate fitness buff to do?

Would you believe an intense workout without weights? Yes, even advanced bodybuilders who toy with the big Olympic iron can have a decent muscle-building session without anything but a chair, a bath towel and their own bodyweight. And we're not just talking about a maintenance program here; this is a real body*building* regimen. Work these exercises hard, and you will stimulate real muscle growth.

One-legged squat

Sissy squat

One-legged calf raise

Feet-elevated pushup

Door row

Towel lateral raise

Crunch

That's it—seven exercises to cover the entire body. Sets and reps? That's up to you, but remember, many of these exercises constitute new stresses on your muscular structures. If it's been a while since you've worked out, one comfortable set of each exercise is plenty. This should minimize the achy aftereffects. If you've been training for months or even years, you can still get a fantastic workout with just one set of each exercise taken to the limit, but advanced folks should go by feel. If you don't get a good muscle ache from one set, try two or three. And be sure to flex the worked muscle group after each set for even better results.

All the exercises are relatively simple in this routine, but in case you're not familiar with some of these movements, here's a description of each:

> *One-legged squat.* Stand on a stable chair (in a doorway, if possible), with the back of the chair on the same side of your body as the leg you are going to work. Hold the other leg out to the side and let it hang freely throughout the set. Bend your working leg slowly while keeping your torso perpendicular to the floor. Use the sides of the doorway for balance if you need to. Continue down into the low squat position, then push back up to the top. Once you've done as many reps as you can, turn yourself 180 degrees and work the other leg. If there's no chair around, these can also be done on the floor with the nonworking leg held forward (extended in front of you). Next to barbell squats, the one-legged squat is undoubtedly one of the best thigh burners around.

> *Sissy squat.* Stand with the back of the chair at your side and hold onto it with one hand for balance. Come up on your toes and begin leaning your torso back while bending at the knees. Go down as far as possible *while keeping your torso and thighs on the same plane*—no bending at the waist. When you reach a comfortable low position (you'll look like you're doing the limbo) pull yourself up with your frontal thigh muscles and repeat. This will really work both the inner and outer quads. You can vary your sets by keeping the knees together on one set and the knees angled out on the following set.

One-legged calf raise. Stand back about two feet from a wall. Lean your entire body toward the wall until your chest is only a few inches from it. Raise one foot off of the floor, and while keeping the torso and legs in a straight line, begin doing one-legged calf raises. You'll feel a good stretch and a great contraction from each rep. When you hit failure, shake your calf out and repeat with the other leg.

Feet-elevated pushup. Assume the regular pushup position, with hands slightly wider than shoulder-width, but instead of having your feet on the ground, have your feet elevated on a chair or the edge of a bed. From here, begin doing pushups. Continue until failure. The higher your feet are elevated, the harder these are. If you've got a couple of phone books, put one under each hand to give you a more complete range of motion. You'll feel this exercise through your entire upper body, especially in your pecs, triceps and delts.

Door row. Roll a towel up and grab it with both hands around the middle leaving about six inches between your thumbs. Put this"gap" against the edge of a half-open door and loop the ends of the towel around the knobs on each side. Slide your grip down to the end of the towel and place your feet next to the door. Lean your torso down and back and bend at your knees into a squat position—thighs parallel with the floor—arms extended. Stay in this squat position and begin rowing your bodyweight while leaning back and keeping your torso angled away from the door. Pull yourself up until your chest meets your hands and flex your back muscles. You can control the amount of resistance by altering the angle of your torso (how much you lean back).

Towel lateral raise. This exercise pits one deltoid against the other. Grab each end of a rolled-up towel, one end in the right hand and one end in the left, about

2 1/2 feet between thumbs. As you pull up with one arm, resist with the other. In effect, this becomes a set of alternate lateral raises. And what an effective set it is; every rep is a near-maximum effort. Another plus: Because the resistance is pulling down on the thumbside of each hand, your arm is in the perfect position for lateral-delt work. You'll have a full deltoid pump before you can say "cantaloupes."

Crunch. Lie on your back on the floor, bend your legs at a 90-degree angle and place your lower legs on the seat of a chair. From here, put your hands behind your head and curl your upper back and head off of the floor as you exhale; your lower back should remain in contact with the floor. In the contracted position, blow the last bit of air out of your lungs and crunch the abs hard. Release, inhale, lie back and repeat. Remember, the range of motion of this exercise is only a few inches, just enough to contract the abdominals.

This routine hits just about every muscle group hard, with almost no equipment necessary. That means you can use it on vacation, at the office or when you just need a change of pace from your usual weight workout. It's perfect for the times you need a quick, invigorating pump and there simply aren't any barbells and dumbbells available.

If you're away from equipment for long periods, you can always use this program as a stand-alone bodybuilding routine to keep you fit and well-muscled. Use your imagination along with some of the intensity techniques discussed in chapter 5, and you'll get even faster results. For example, you could do each set in superslow fashion—10 seconds up (positive) and two seconds down (negative)—for a superintense, growth-stimulating workout.

No matter how you choose to use it or what your level of development, the weight-free workout is but one more valuable weapon in your ever-growing fitness arsenal. To vary a popular quotation: Use it so you don't lose it, even if there's not a barbell or dumbbell in sight.

10

There's No Place Like Home

Dorothy was right: There is no place like home—especially for training to be the best you can be. Whether you're a beginner (male or female), an athlete (pro or amateur) or an advanced bodybuilder, a home gym can help you drive forward in your pursuit of muscle, power and enhanced athletic ability.

The home gym is a definite time-saver, a worthwhile investment and, most of all, a healthy convenience that can help you cut out the time-wasting nonessentials of your workout. In the latter respect, it's comparable to a VCR: With a VCR, you watch TV when it's convenient, easily able to fast-forward through the commercials; with a home gym...well, you get the idea.

Here's a quick overview of the key principles espoused in this book:

> *Efficiency.* The techniques, tips and suggestions in the preceding chapters are all intended to help you formulate a practical, effective training strategy with as little waste as possible (efficiency of effort).

> *Individuality.* This is not a cookbook per se. The routines, training cycles and intensity levels are merely samples. Feel free to adapt them to your specific body type, genetic potential and time constraints. Do, however, always stick to the basic principles in this book, such as phase training and proper utilization of intensity.

> *Intensity.* Hard, all-out training is the name of the game when it comes to rapid increases in size and strength.

The more intensely you train, the more you will gain, as long as you don't overrun your recovery ability.

Recovery ability. You must monitor your progress, especially when training intensely. If gains stagnate and you begin to feel listless, you probably need less intensity, less training or even a seven-to-10-day layoff. Keep Seyle's General Adaptation Syndrome (alarm, resistance, exhaustion) in mind, and always work with a phase approach to keep progress at optimum levels.

Variation. Boredom with your workout indicates a need for something fresh—some type of variance to make the workout more interesting and more productive, such as new exercises or the incorporation of new intensity techniques. When it comes to working out, don't be afraid of change. Remember, we strive for order, but we thrive on change.

Goals. Whether you want more tone, shape, power or muscle mass, the home gym can help you achieve it. Simply govern your intensity and use a strategic training approach, and you will reach your bodybuilding goals.

Discipline. No matter what your aspirations, stick to your training with commitment and persistence, and you will gain above and beyond your expectations.

Now that you're armed with an efficient strategy, equip your gym with the right tools, get psyched and start constructing some homegrown muscle.

11

Recommended Reading List

The Health For Life Training Advisor. Everything from overtraining to isometrics to training for sports is discussed in detail: $29.95. Available from Health For Life, 8033 Sunset Blvd., Suite 483, Los Angeles, CA 90046; 1-800-874-5339 or in California 1-800-523-9983.

Super Squats: How to Gain 30 Pounds of Muscle in 6 Weeks. Randall J. Strossen, Ph.D. gives history and information on bodybuilding's king of the mass movements: $12.95 plus $2 postage and handling. Available from IronMind Enterprises Inc., P.O. Box 884, Larkspur, CA 94939; or call *IRONMAN* Books at 1-800-447-0008.

Keys to the Inner Universe. Over 600 pages of exercise descriptions and techniques by Bill Pearl: $35 plus $2.50 shipping and handling. Available from *IRONMAN* Books, P.O. Box 1444, Venice, CA 90291; 1-800-447-0008.

Super High-Intensity Bodybuilding. Ellington Darden, Ph.D., and Director of Research for Nautilus Sports/Medical Industries, instructs you on growth zone training: $11.95 plus $2.50 shipping and handling. Available from *IRONMAN* Books, P.O. Box 1444, Venice, CA 90291; 1-800-447-0008.

Forever Natural. Dave Tuttle gives a motivational account of how to be your athletic best without drugs: $14.95 plus $2.50 shipping and handling. Available from Forever Natural, P.O. Box 2307, Venice, CA 90294; 1-800-252-BOOK. Also Available through *IRONMAN* Books, P.O. Box 1444, Venice, CA 90291; 1-800-447-0008.

Massive Muscles in 10 Weeks. Ellington Darden, Ph.D., discusses more details on how a basic routine can build maximum mass fast: $11.95 plus $2.50 shipping and handling. Available from *IRONMAN* Books, P.O. Box 1444, Venice, CA 90291; 1-800-447-0008.

Secrets of Advanced Bodybuilders. Training information to help you develop the optimum workout: $24.95 plus $2.50 shipping and handling. Available from Health For Life, 8033 Sunset Blvd., Suite 483, Los Angeles, CA 90046; 1-800-874-5339 or in California 1-800-523-9983.

The Human Fuel Handbook. One of the most complete books on nutrition ever written: $29.95 plus $2.50 shipping and handling. Available from Health For Life, 8033 Sunset Blvd., Suite 483, Los Angeles, CA 90046; 1-800-874-5339 or in California 1-800-523-9983. Also available from *IRONMAN* Books 1-800-447-0008.

The Hardgainer. A bimonthly magazine devoted to hard-gaining bodybuilders. For a one-year subscription, send $25 check or money order to The Hardgainer, P.O. Box 8186, Nicosia, Cyprus.

IRONMAN magazine. The number-one independent bodybuilding magazine. Each issue is full of training information, nutrition advice and the best and photography available. For a one-year subscription (12 issues) send $29.95 check or money order to *IRONMAN*, P.O. Box 777, Santa Monica, CA 90406-9930.

Glossary

Compound exercise. Any multiple-joint movement that uses more than one muscle group to move the resistance. In the bench press, for example, you use your deltoids and triceps as well as your pectorals (chest) to move the barbell.

Cycle. One exercise immediately followed by another with no rest in between. For example, using pre-exhaustion for the thighs, you would cycle leg extensions with squats.

Efficiency of effort. Maximum gains with minimal time expenditure.

Hardgainer. Any individual with small bones, a fast metabolism and below-average genetics who finds it extremely hard to put on muscular bodyweight. Hardgainers require special training considerations for best results.

Intensity. The degree of effort used to accomplish a task.

Isolation exercise. Any single-joint movement that primarily uses one muscle group to move the resistance. The barbell curl, for example, is an isolation exercise for the biceps; almost all of the work during a strict barbell curl is performed by the biceps. (Note: Pure isolation is impossible; in other words, even strict isolation exercises employ other muscle groups to a degree.)

Negative portion of a repetition. The half of a rep where you are lowering the resistance. Muscles are stronger in the the negative portion than the positive portion of a rep.

Overtraining. Doing so much work that the body's metabolic system cannot cope (recover) sufficiently.

Phase training. Interspersing weeks of low-intensity training with weeks of high-intensity training. This concept is based on Dr. Hans Selye's General Adaptation Syndrome, which concludes that the body copes with stress in three stages: alarm, resistance and exhaustion. Exhaustion should be avoided for as long as possible.

Positions of flexion. The three positions a muscle should be worked through—midrange, stretch and contracted—for complete *advanced* development.

Positive portion of a repetition. The half of a rep where you are lifting the resistance.

Pre-exhaustion. Immediately following an isolation exercise with a compound movement for the same target muscle group in order push the bodypart harder. For example, a pre-exhaustion cycle for the shoulders would be lateral raises followed immediately by overhead presses. The laterals isolate the deltoids, and then the presses bring in the triceps to help the deltoids continue contracting. Other examples include thighs: leg extensions/squats; chest: dumbbell flyes/bench presses; back: pullovers/chinups.

Range of motion. The total possible movement of any exercise from start to finish, stretch to contraction.

Recovery ability. Your metabolism's ability to adapt (recover) from work.

Repetition. One complete movement of an exercise including both positive and negative (up and down).

Set. A continuous performance of successive repetitions.

Specialization. Favoring a weak, lagging muscle group, with the proper adjustments to the rest of your routine, in order for this bodypart to "catch up" in development and strength.

Training log. An ongoing diary of your workouts, complete with exercises, sets, reps, poundages and intensity techniques used.

Training to failure. Pushing a set of repetitions until it is impossible to do another rep.

Warmup set. A set of reps of a particular exercise done with lighter poundage to get the muscles ready for heavier work.

APPENDIX A
Home Gym Checklists

Basic Equipment

_ 12' x 12' area (or at least 7' x 7')

_ 110-pound metal barbell/dumbbell set (rubber coated, if possible)

_ Extra weight (four 25s; this extra poundage is optional for women trainees)

_ A comfortable, adjustable bench with uprights and leg extension/leg curl

_ Calf block

_ Chinning bar (optional for women)

_ Lifting belt

_ Lifting gloves

_ Weight belt (optional for women)

Add-ons

_ Extra regular plates (two to four more of each: 25s or 50s, 10s, 5s, 2 1/2s)

_ EZ-curl bar

_ Dumbbell bars (one to two extra pairs)

_ Barbell bar (one extra)

_ Dipping bars (optional)

_ Pulldown machine (optional)

_ Power rack or squat stands (optional)

_ Olympic set (optional, but recommended for power rack use)

Productivity Items

_ Training log

_ Accessory rack

_ Gym clock

_ Bulletin board

_ Full-length mirror

APPENDIX B
Exercise Descriptions

Alternating lunge *(frontal thighs, hamstrings, buttocks)*. Stand erect with a barbell across your shoulders. Step out about two feet in front of you with your right foot, bend your right knee until you're in a lunge position and your left knee touches the floor. From here, push back to the starting position (feet together) with your right leg and repeat with your left. Continue alternating legs throughout the set. Tip: For a different version of this, you can step back with the nonworking leg while slowly bending the working leg. Touch the nonworking leg's knee to the floor, drive back up to the starting position and repeat with the other leg.

Barbell curl *(biceps)*. Stand upright with a loaded barbell at arm's length. Slowly curl the bar up to your shoulders without swinging the body, and be sure to keep your elbows as stationary as possible at your sides. Tip: Lean slightly forward to keep resistance on the biceps throughout the movement. Alternate exercises: seated dumbbell curl, alternate dumbbell curl.

Behind-the-neck chin *(back—latissimus dorsi)*. Take a slightly wider-than-shoulder-width grip on the chinning bar and pull yourself up until the back of your neck touches the bar. Lower and repeat. Tip: At the top, really squeeze your shoulder blades together to affect the middle back as well as the lats.

Behind-the-neck press *(deltoids)*. Take a loaded barbell off a rack onto your shoulders as if you were about to do squats. Sit on a bench, plant your feet on the floor and press the barbell overhead. Lower the bar to the back of your neck and repeat. Tip: don't pause at the bottom. Also, try a set without locking out on any of the reps. Alternate exercise: standing barbell press, seated dumbbell press.

Bench press *(chest)*. Recline on a bench with a loaded bar on the racks. Take a slightly wider-than-shoulder-width grip on the bar, lift it off of the racks and lower to your middle chest area. Without a pause, ram the bar back to arm's length and repeat. When doing this exercise, you should always have someone standing by in case you miss. Tip: To get an even greater stretch in the pecs, keep your elbows out away from your body and touch the bar to the base of your neck. Alternate exercise: dumbbell bench press.

Bent-over barbell row *(midback)*. Bend at your waist, grab a loaded barbell with a slightly wider-than-shoulder-width grip and pull the bar to your lower ribcage. Keep your elbows angled out away from your sides and don't raise your torso above parallel to the floor. Tip: Try a set with an underhand grip and your arms close to your body to bring the lower lats into play. Alternate exercises: one-arm dumbbell row (a better exercise for those with low-back problems), incline dumbbell row (face down on an incline bench).

Crunch *(abdominals)*. Recline on your back on the floor with your lower legs supported on an exercise bench (legs bent at a 90-degree angle). Roll up until your upper back is off of the floor, blow the air out of your lungs and contract the abs hard. Uncurl the body, inhale and repeat. Tip: Keep the lower back against the ground at all times. Alternate exercise: none.

Decline flye *(lower chest)*. Set one end of your bench up on your calf block (making sure it's sturdy and won't flip over). Grab a dumbbell in each hand and recline on the bench with your head at the lower end. Press the dumbbells over your chest and lower them down and back with a slight, constant bend in your elbows. When you feel a good stretch in your pecs, raise the dumbbells up over the chest like you were hugging a tree and repeat. Tip: Squeeze the pecs at the top for two seconds.

Decline reverse wrist curl *(forearm extensors)*. With one end of your bench on your calf block, take a close, *overhand* grip on a loaded barbell and rest your forearms on the *low* end of the bench, hands hanging off the end. From here, curl the bar up as high as possible and flex the forearm extensor muscles on the top of your lower arm. Lower and repeat.

Decline wrist curl *(forearm flexors)*. With one end of your bench on your calf block, take a close, underhand grip on a loaded barbell and rest your forearms on the *low* end of the bench, hands hanging off the end. From here, curl the bar up as high as possible and flex the inner forearm muscles. Lower and repeat.

Dip (elbows in) *(triceps)*. Get up on your dipping bars with your arms locked. From here, bend your arms, keeping them close to the body and your head up. When you reach the bottom, reverse your motion, drive back to the top position and repeat. Tip: Flex the triceps hard in the top position of every rep.

Dip (elbows out) *(chest)*. Support yourself with locked arms on your dipping bars. With your chin on your chest, lower slowly to the bottom position, keeping your elbows out away from your body. You should feel a stretch in your pectorals. Without a pause, drive back to the top position. Tip: Really squeeze your pecs in the top position to get your mind in touch with the muscles being worked.

Donkey calf raise *(calves)*. Bend at the waist, torso 90 degrees to the thighs, and rest your forearms on a table, high bench or racked barbell bar. With the balls of your feet up on your calf block, have your training partner sit on your hips. Do calf raises until failure. Tip: If you train solo, you can still do donkeys by hanging weight around your hips with a weight belt.

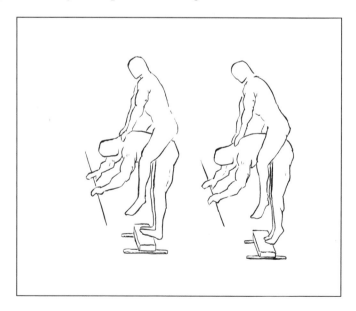

Feet-elevated pushup *(chest)*. This is a very effective exercise, but there's really no way to add weight. This means that when you reach the upper-rep range, you may want to switch to the bench press. Get in the standard pushup position and elevate your feet on your bench. With a hand spacing a little wider than shoulder-width, keep your elbows out and touch your chest to the floor. If you keep your head up, you will work more of the middle and lower chest. Tip: Place something the thickness of a phone book under each hand in order to get a better stretch in the pectorals (Note: You can buy pushup bars at most sporting goods stores.) Alternate exercises: parallel-bar dip (elbows out), bench press.

Freehand calf raise *(calves)*. Begin doing calf raises—using both feet—in rapid fashion until your calves "burn out." Do the reps as fast as possible without using momentum, and be prepared for a few seconds of cramping. Tip: Lean forward against a wall for a better stretch.

Incline barbell press *(upper chest)*. Recline on a 35-degree incline bench with a loaded barbell on the racks behind you. Take a grip a little wider than shoulder-width on the bar, palms facing forward, and unrack the weight. From this arms-extended position over your chest, lower the bar to your clavicles and without a pause drive it back to the top and then repeat. Tip: To get a real burn in the upper pecs, don't lock out at the top of your reps; simply drive up to the two-thirds position and then repeat.

Incline dumbbell curl *(biceps)*. Recline on a 45-degree incline bench with a dumbbell in each hand. From a dead-hang position, curl the dumbbells up to your shoulders simultaneously with as little upper-arm movement as possible. Lower to the stretch position and repeat. Tip: Supinating your hands will help contract the biceps more fully. To do this, start with the palms facing each other in the dead-hang position. As you curl the dumbbells, begin to turn your palms up. In the top contracted position, try to turn the little fingers over as far as possible. Lower and repeat.

Incline dumbbell press *(upper chest)*. Use a 35-degree incline bench for these. Curl/clean the dumbbells up to your shoulders, recline on the bench and start pressing. Drive the dumbbells up to arm's length above your eyes. Keep your elbows away from your body on the way down. Tip: Try one set with the palms facing each

126

other and the next set with palms facing forward for more complete upper-pec development. Also, always keep your lower back flat against the bench. Alternate exercise: incline barbell press.

Incline flye *(upper chest).* Take a dumbbell in each hand and recline on a 35-degree incline bench. Press the dumbbells over your chest. While keeping only a slight bend in your elbows, lower the dumbbells down and back until they are on the same plane as the deltoids. Raise the bells back to the starting position with your elbows still slightly bent, as though you were hugging a tree, using pec power alone, then repeat. Tip: Flex your upper-chest muscles at the top of every rep.

Incline one-arm lateral raise *(deltoids).* These are done by sitting sideways on an incline bench. You lean one shoulder against the bench while you work your other shoulder with a one-arm lateral raise. This incline allows the delt to get a full stretch in the bottom position. Tip: Keep the dumbbell parallel with the floor at all times.

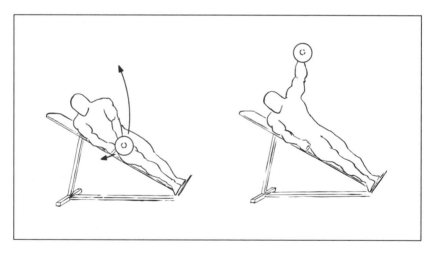

Incline reverse wrist curl *(forearm extensors).* With one end of your bench up on your calf block, take a close, *overhand* grip on a loaded barbell and rest your forearms on the *high* end of the bench, hands hanging off the end. From here, curl the bar up until your hands are almost perpendicular to the floor. Lower all the way down and repeat.

Incline wrist curl *(forearm flexors)*. With one end of your bench up on your calf block, take a close, underhand grip on a loaded barbell and rest your forearms on the *high* end of the bench, hands hanging off the end. From here, curl the bar up until your hands are almost perpendicular to the floor. Lower all the way down and repeat.

Kickback *(triceps)*. Take a dumbbell in each hand and bend at the waist until your torso is parallel to the floor. With your upper arms next to your sides—arms at 90-degree angles—extend your forearms back and contract your triceps (your arms should be parallel with the floor in the top position). Lower the dumbbells, keeping your upper arms stationary and repeat. Tip: Try one set with palms facing your thighs and one set with palms facing up.

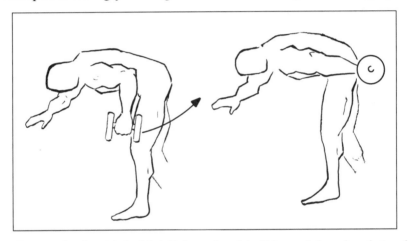

Lateral raise *(deltoids)*. Take a dumbbell in each hand and stand erect with the dumbbells in front of your thighs, palms facing each other. Raise the dumbbells out from your sides with slightly bent arms until the 'bells are at shoulder level. Here you should feel a contraction in the side delt heads. Lower and repeat. Tip: Watch the position of the dumbbells; keep them parallel to the floor. If the front of the dumbbell is higher than the rear, your front deltoid will be getting the brunt of the work.

Leg curl *(hamstrings)*. Load your leg curl apparatus, lie face-down on your bench and place the back of your lower leg against the roller pads. From here, curl your lower legs up, keeping your feet flexed toward your legs, until the pads touch your buttocks. Hold for a count of two, lower and repeat. Tip: Support your upper body on your elbows to prevent too much hip movement.

Leg extension *(frontal thighs)*. Load your leg extension apparatus, sit down and hook your feet under the roller pads—knees should be bent at 90-degree angles. With your torso at a 90-degree angle to the thighs, extend the lower leg until your knees lock and your quadriceps contract. Hold this position for a count of two, lower and repeat. Tip: Keep your toes turned in for more outer-thigh development (sweep) or toes angled out for lower- and inner-thigh development.

Lying triceps dumbbell extension *(triceps)*. Take a dumbbell in each hand and lie back on a flat bench. With the dumbbells over your chest in the arm-extended position, palms facing each other lower the 'bells down in an arc to each ear while keeping your elbows as close together as possible (without hitting yourself in the face with the dumbbells). Then drive them back up to the beginning position and repeat. Tip: Keep the upper arms as stationary as possible and angled slightly back for more tension on the triceps.

Lying triceps extension *(triceps)*. Lie back on a bench and press a loaded barbell up over your chest with a close grip (eight inches between thumbs). While keeping your upper arms as stationary as possible, lower the bar and touch it to your forehead, or to the bench behind your head, whichever is more comfortable while keeping your elbows as close together as possible. Drive the bar back over your chest in an arc and repeat. Tip: Keep the upper arms parallel and angled slightly back throughout the movement. Alternate exercise: Overhead triceps extension.

Military press *(deltoids)*. Clean a loaded barbell bar to your shoulders. From here, keep your torso as upright as possible and press the bar overhead. Lower to neck level and repeat. Tip: Try going only two-thirds of the way up on your reps for continuous tension on your delts.

One-arm bent-over dumbbell row *(back)*. Take a dumbbell in one hand, bend at the waist with your arm hanging straight down, your other arm supported on the bench. Pull the dumbbell up to your shoulder, bending your elbows and keeping your palm facing inward (toward the bench). Lower and repeat. Work each side separately. Tip: Try a set with the palm facing back for more midback involvement. Alternate exercise: bent-over barbell row.

One-arm nonsupport concentration curl *(biceps)*. Take a dumbbell in one hand, bend at the waist with your arm hanging straight down. Curl the dumbbell up to your shoulder, keeping your torso and upper arm as motionless as possible. Lower and repeat. Work each arm separately. Tip: Try the supination technique mentioned in the incline dumbbell curl description on these as well.

One-legged calf raise *(calves)*. Hold a dumbbell in your hand on the same side as the calf you are working or secure a sufficient amount of poundage around your waist with a weight belt (see chapter 2 for instructions on how to build a good calf block). Grasp one of your bench uprights with your free hand for support, place the ball of your foot on your calf block and begin doing repetitions. Tip: Try to rise with more pressure on the big-toe side of the foot for inner-calf stimulation. Alternate exercises: donkey calf raise, standing calf raise.

One-legged Squat *(frontal thighs, buttocks, hamstrings)*. Don't pass this movement off as an easy exercise. It's tough and will jolt your thighs into rapid growth when pushed to failure. For one-legged squats, raise your bench press racks to about shoulder height and place a bar across them. Then stand up on the bench, balance on one leg while holding onto the bar for stability and squat, letting the resting leg dangle freely beside the bench. Tip: Try to keep the

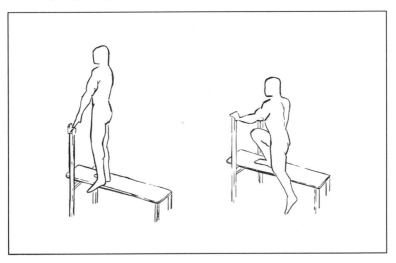

torso upright, and when you're able to get 15 reps, add weight by holding a dumbbell or barbell plate in your hand on the same side of the body as your working leg. Also, if you're too weak in the beginning, help yourself complete the required number of reps by pulling up with your arms or try an alternate movement. Alternate exercises: barbell squat, front squat.

Overhead extension *(triceps).* This is best done with an EZ-curl bar. Grab the bar in the middle position, thumbs about six inches apart. Press the bar overhead. From this overhead position, lower the bar back behind your head, while keeping the upper arms as stationary as possible. When you reach the stretch position, reverse the movement and press the bar back overhead.

Pullover *(back—latissimus dorsi).* Recline on a flat bench with your head hanging off of one end and a loaded EZ-curl bar on the floor behind you. Grab the bar with a shoulder-width grip, palms facing up. With your arms bent, pull the bar up to your chest, keeping it about two inches from your face. Touch your upper chest with it, lower to the floor and repeat. Tip: Hook your feet around the legs of the bench for better stability. You can also do this exercise with stiff arms, but don't lower the bar too far past the level of the bench or you could injure your shoulders.

Reverse crunch *(abdominals).* Lie on the ground, bend your knees and cross your feet at the ankles. Open your legs until the sides of your thighs are almost touching the floor. With your arms at your sides and hands flat on the ground, curl your knees toward your chest. Your hips will come off the ground a few inches as you "roll up" in the finish position. Lower your legs, touch your feet to the floor and repeat. Tip: Blow the air out of your lungs in the finish position to get a more intense abdominal contraction.

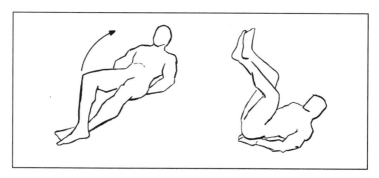

Reverse curl *(forearm extensors, biceps)*. Do regular standing barbell curls but use an overhand grip on the bar instead of an undergrip. This exercise will work the entire forearm area plus the brachialis, a muscle located between the biceps and triceps on the outer, upper arm.

Reverse curl *(forearm extensors, biceps)*. Take an overhand, shoulder-width grip on a loaded barbell bar. Stand erect and curl the bar to the shoulders. Lower and repeat. Tip: You can also use an EZ-curl bar on these for a slightly different effect.

Seated dumbbell curl *(biceps)*. Sit on the end of a flat bench with a dumbbell in each hand. With palms facing forward, curl the dumbbells up simultaneously until they reach your shoulders. Lower and repeat. Tip: Supinate the hands as you curl. To do this, start the movement with your palms facing each other, and as you curl, rotate the hands, turning the little fingers up when you reach the top.

Seated dumbbell press *(deltoids)*. Sit on the end of a bench and curl/clean a pair of dumbbells to your shoulders. With the dumbbells resting on your shoulders, press them simultaneously overhead while keeping your palms facing forward. Try to stay upright, with as little back arch as possible. Lower slowly. Tip: You can also try alternate dumbbell presses—one dumbbell is lowered as the other is raised. This will keep your cheating to a minimum. Alternate exercise: behind-the-neck press, military press.

Sissy squat *(frontal thighs)*. Hold onto an upright with one hand and bend your knees while keeping the thighs and torso on the same plane (don't bend at the waist). Lean back as far as possible. (At

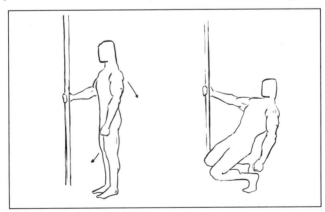

the bottom you'll be in a limbo dance position.) By doing this, your knees will go forward, and you will get a tremendous stretch in the thighs when you get to the bottom position. Tip: Put a 2" x 4" (board) under your heels for balance and hold a plate on your chest with your free hand when you get strong enough. Alternate exercises: Leg extension, lunge.

Squat *(frontal thighs, buttocks, lower back, hamstrings).* This exercise is a bit more dangerous than one-legged squats in the home gym setting, but with the right precautions it's one of the best movements around. Take a loaded barbell off of a rack and onto your shoulders. Back away from the rack, take a comfortable stance and squat until your thighs are just below parallel to the floor. You may want to put a 2" x 4" plank under your heels for better form and balance. Also, throughout the movement be sure to look straight ahead to prevent rounding or arching of the lower back, and keep your torso as upright as possible to maximize thigh involvement. If you're going all out on these, have a partner standing by in case you miss. Tip: Squat while straddling your exercise bench to get the right depth. This is also safer if you miss because you can sit and rest until you can get to the top to rerack the weight.

Standing calf raise *(calves).* With a loaded barbell bar across your shoulders, stand up on your calf block near a wall, feet about 12 inches apart. Lean forward and balance by placing the top of your head against the wall (a towel would be helpful here). Proceed to do calf raises, going up as high as possible and down as low as possible. Tip: You can also do these with a loaded weight belt around your waist instead of a barbell bar across your shoulders.

Stiff-legged deadlift on bench *(hamstrings, lower back, buttocks).* The stiff-legged deadlift really hits the lower back and hamstrings hard, not to mention the buttocks. Load a bar on your bench's racks, stand up on the bench, lift the bar and take a step back. With the bar at arm's length, slowly bend at the waist, keeping the bar close to the legs. When the bar is about five inches from hitting the bench, reverse your motion and slowly pull your torso into the upright position. Tip: One hand over and the other under (over-under grip) will make the bar more secure and keep it from slipping. Alternate exercise: The leg curl can be used as a substitute, but it doesn't work your lower back as the deadlift does.

Toes-pointed leg curl *(calves, hamstrings)*. These are done just like regular leg curls, only you point your toes away from your legs. This brings the calves into play.

Undergrip chin *(biceps, back)*. Grab the chinning bar, palms facing back, with a shoulder-width grip. From a dead-hang position, pull yourself up until your clavicles touch the bar. Lower and repeat. Tip: Keep your head back, especially at the top, to get a better contraction in the biceps.

Upright dumbbell row *(deltoids)*. Take a dumbbell in each hand and stand erect. With your palms facing back, pull the dumbbells up to chest level while keeping them close to your body. Lower and repeat. Tip: Keep your hands slightly wider than shoulder-width to ensure lateral (side) delt head work.

Wide-grip chin *(back—latissimus dorsi)*. Take a grip about a hand-width out from shoulder-width on each side. Pull up, arch your lower back slightly and touch your clavicles to the bar. Tip: You can use a chair under your feet for assisted reps after you hit failure. Also, by keeping your feet on the chair throughout your set, you can more easily keep the back arched for a better latissimus contraction. Just don't cheat. Alternate exercise: pulldowns.

Wide-grip upright row *(deltoids)*. Use a slightly wider-than-shoulder-width grip on these. While standing upright with the barbell hanging at arm's length, pull the bar up to the chest. Keep it close to your body. Stop at midchest level, lower slowly and repeat. If this exercise hurts your wrists or shoulders, use dumbbells for less joint restriction. Tip: Try using a lighter weight once in a while and raising the bar to your nose instead of stopping at your chest. Alternate exercise: dumbbell upright row, dumbbell lateral raise (standing or seated).

Wide-grip upright row to nose *(deltoids)*. Grab a loaded barbell with a slightly wider-than-shoulder-width grip and stand erect with it. From arm's length—bar in front of the thighs—pull the bar up to your nose. Lower and repeat.

Wrist curl *(forearm flexors)*. Take a close, underhand grip on a loaded barbell and rest your forearms on your flat bench, hands hanging off the end. From here, curl the bar up and flex the inner forearm muscles. Lower slowly and repeat.

(Note: For more exercise descriptions, get a copy of Bill Pearl's *Keys to the Inner Universe*. This text gives a description of almost every exercise in existence and is indispensable for the beginner as well as the advanced weight trainer. See the recommended reading list.)

APPENDIX C
Training Itineraries

Break-in Through Intermediate Itineraries

Break-in (6 wks.)	*1st week*	EOE routine; one set per exercise; stop each set well before failure.
	2nd week	EOE routine; one set per exercise; each set (except warmups) to failure
	3rd week	Full EOE routine; all sets (except warmups) to failure.
Beginner's Itinerary (6-month cycle)	*1st six weeks*	EOE routine; all sets (except warmups) to failure.
	Next two weeks	EOE routine; stop all sets one to two reps prior to failure.
	Next six weeks	EOE routine; all sets (except warmups) to failure.
	Next two weeks	EOE routine; stop all sets one to two reps prior to failure.
	Next six weeks	EOE routine; all sets (except warmups) to failure. Introduce intensity techniques with caution.
	Next two weeks	EOE routine; stop all sets one to two reps prior to failure.
Intermediate Itinerary (6-month specialization cycle)	*1st four weeks*	Work specialization into your EOE routine for your weakest bodypart. Use intensity techniques sparingly.
	Next two weeks	Normal EOE routine; stop each set short of positive failure.
	Next four weeks	Specialization on a different weak bodypart. Use intensity techniques sparingly.
	Next two weeks	Normal EOE routine; stop each set short of positive failure.
	Next four weeks	Specialization on a weak bodypart. Use intensity techniques sparingly
	Next two weeks	Normal EOE routine; stop each set short of positive failure.
	Next four weeks	Specialization on a weak bodypart. Use intensity techniques sparingly.
	Next two weeks	Normal EOE routine; stop each set short of positive failure.

Advanced Itinerary

Advanced Itinerary (4 1/2-month cycle)	1st four weeks	POF routine; all sets to positive failure only.
	Next two weeks	POF routine; stop each set before positive failure.
	Next four weeks	POF routine; use intensity techniques cautiously.
	Next two weeks	POF routine; stop each set before positive failure.
	Next four weeks	POF routine; use intensity techniques cautiously.
	Next two weeks	POF routine; stop each set before positive failure.
Intermediate Itinerary (4 1/2-month specialization cycle)		Work specialization into your EOE routine for your weakest bodypart. Use intensity techniques sparingly.
		Normal EOE routine; stop each set short of positive failure.
		Specialization on a different weak bodypart. Use intensity techniques sparingly.
		Normal EOE routine; stop each set short of positive failure.
		Specialization on a weak bodypart. Use intensity techniques sparingly
		Normal EOE routine; stop each set short of positive failure.

Advanced Itinerary for a 4 1/2-month cycle

Intermediate Itinerary for a 4 1/2-month cycle

Advanced Itinerary for a 4 1/2-month cycle

Intermediate Itinerary for a 4 1/2-month cycle

Continue alternating Intermediate and Advanced Itineraries for 4 1/2-month cycles

Athlete's Itinerary

Break-in (6 wks.)	*1st two week*	Athlete's EOE routine; one set per exercise; stop each set well before failure.
	3rd week	Athlete's EOE routine; one set per exercise; each set (except warmups) to failure
Beginner's Itinerary (6-month cycle)	*1st six weeks*	Athlete's EOE routine; set total up to required number (nine to 18); all sets (except warmups) to failure.
	Next two weeks	Athlete's EOE routine; stop all sets one to two reps prior to failure.
	Next six weeks	Athlete's EOE routine; all sets (except warmups) to failure.
	Next two weeks	Athlete's EOE routine; stop all sets one to two reps prior to failure.
	Next six weeks	Athlete's EOE routine; all sets (except warmups) to failure. Introduce intensity techniques with caution—no more than four total sets per workout.
	Next two weeks	Athlete's EOE routine; stop all sets one to two reps prior to failure.
Intermediate Itinerary (6-month specialization cycle)	*1st four weeks*	Work specialization into your EOE routine for a chosen bodypart. Use intensity techniques sparingly.
	Next two weeks	Normal athlete's EOE routine; stop each set short of positive failure.
	Next four weeks	Specialization on a different bodypart. Use intensity techniques sparingly.
	Next two weeks	Normal athlete's EOE routine; stop each set short of positive failure.
	Next four weeks	Specialization on a chosen bodypart. Use intensity techniques sparingly.
	Next two weeks	Normal athlete's EOE routine; stop each set short of positive failure.
	Next four weeks	Specialization on a chosen bodypart. Use intensity techniques sparingly.
	Next two weeks	Normal athlete's EOE routine; stop each set short of positive failure.

APPENDIX D
Alternate Routines

Alternate EOE Routine (Mon., Wed., Fri.)

Thighs	Front squat	2 x 10-15
	Leg extension	1 x 10-15
Hamstrings	Leg curl	2 x 10-15
Chest	Incline dumbbell press	2 x 8-12
	Decline barbell press	1 x 8-12
Back	Behind-the neck chinup	2 x 8-12
	Incline dumbbell row	1 x 8-12
Shoulders	Behind-the-neck press	2 x 8-12
	Dumbbell lateral raise	2 x 8-12
Calves	Donkey calf raise	3 x 12-20
Triceps	Close-grip bench press	1 x 8-12
Biceps	Undergrip chin	1 x 8-12
Abs	Reverse crunch	2 x 15-25

Alternate Condensed EOE Routine (Mon. & Thurs.)

Thighs	Front squat	2 x 10-15
Hamstrings	Leg curl	2 x 10-15
Chest	Incline dumbbell press	2 x 8-12
Back	Behind-the-neck chinup	2 x 8-12
	Incline dumbbell row	1 x 8-12
Shoulders	Behind the neck Press	2 x 8-12
	Dumbbell lateral raise	1 x 8-12
Calves	Donkey calf raise	2 x 12-20
Triceps	Close-grip bench press	1 x 8-12
Biceps	Undergrip chin	1 x 8-12
Abs	Reverse crunch	1 x 15-25

Women's Alternate EOE Routine (Mon. & Thurs.)

Thighs, buttocks	Front squat	2 x 10-15
Hamstrings	Leg curl	1 x 10-15
Chest	Pushup (elevated, if possible)	2 x max
Back	Two-arm dumbbell row	2 x 8-12
Shoulders	Press behind the neck	2 x 8-12
Calves	Standing calf raise	2 x 12-20
Abs	Reverse crunch	2 x 10-25

Athlete's Alternate EOE Routine (Mon. & Thurs.)

Thighs	Front squat	1-2 x 10-15
Hamstrings	Leg curl	1-2 x 10-15
Chest	Incline dumbbell press	1-2 x 8-12
Back	Behind-the-neck chinup	1-2 x 8-12
	One-arm dumbbell row	1-2 x 8-12
Shoulders	Behind the neck Press	1-2 x 8-12
	Dumbbell lateral raise	1-2 x 8-12
Calves	Standing calf raise	1-2 x 12-20
Abs	Reverse crunch	1-2 x 12-20

142

INDEX

EZ-curl bar, 34

F

Failure, positive, 54, 83
Failure, training to, 44
Ferrigno, Lou, 16
Forced reps, 67

G

General Adaptation Syndrome, 50, 52, 112
Gironda, Vince, 82
Grimek, John, 15

H

Hardgainer, 48, 92
Home training unit, complete, 38

I

Intensity, 50, 61
   application, 70
   progression, 63
   techniques, 64-69
Intermediate itinerary, 80
IRONMAN magazine, 48
Isolation movements, 65
Isometric exercise, 69
Isometric stops, 68

J

Jones, Arthur, 74, 77
Journal of Applied Physiology, 69

L

LaLanne, Jack, 16
Lee, Bruce, 16

M

McRobert, Stuart, 48
Mentzer, Mike, 67

Mentzer, Ray, 68

N
Nautilus machines, 74
Nautilus Sports/Medical Industries, 66
Negatives, 68
Norris, Chuck, 16

O
Olympic weight set, 38
1 1/4 reps, 67
Overtraining, 61, 70

P
Pearl, Bill, 15
Phase training, 49, 50, 58
   advanced, 95
POF four-day split routine, 91
POF six-day split routine, 92
Positions of flexion, 87-90
Power rack, 35, 36
Pre-exhaustion, 65, 77
Prefatigue, 65
Pulldown machine, 35
Pump, muscle, 63

R
Range of motion, 53, 58
Repetition speed, 53
Rest/pause, 66

S
Schwarzenegger, Arnold, 67
Selye, Dr. Hans, 50
Specialization
   routines, 78-79
Squat stands, 38
Steinborn, Heinrich "Milo," 21

Superslow reps, 66

T

W

HOME GROWN

A GREAT PHYSIQUE WITHOUT ALL THE HASSLE

Weights not included

Free brochure available from *IRONMAN* Products.

$389.95

Price includes shipping

Now you can get the greatest workouts of your life—at home. The IVANKO bench is a sound investment in your muscle-building future, one you'll use for a lifetime. Forget commercial-gym hassles, and get the home-training advantage!